"Very unique perspective for understanding mental health and approach to treatment. Finally there is a practical and scientific perspective for using biblical methods in therapy."

Sania Dookie, *Pediatrics Mental Health Therapist*

"I found it fascinating! I recently started recovery from food addiction and a lot the information was very useful."

Dawn Wooten, *Adjunct Professor*

"The contents of this book is a revolutionary approach to therapy that challenges helping professionals to encapsulate the spiritual, psychological and neurological perspectives to treat mental health disorders."

Rolando A. Hyman, MA, *Canadian Certified Counselor (CCC)*

NEUROPLASTICITY

HEALING THE BRAIN
FROM
PSYCHOLOGICAL
DISORDERS
THROUGH
BIBLICAL MEDITATION

DR. COURTNEY DOOKIE

WESTBOW
PRESS®
A DIVISION OF THOMAS NELSON
& ZONDERVAN

This book is a work of non-fiction. Unless otherwise noted, the author and the publisher make no explicit guarantees as to the accuracy of the information contained in this book and in some cases, names of people and places have been altered to protect their privacy.

WestBow Press books may be ordered through booksellers or by contacting:

WestBow Press
A Division of Thomas Nelson & Zondervan
1663 Liberty Drive
Bloomington, IN 47403
www.westbowpress.com
844-714-3454

Because of the dynamic nature of the Internet, any web addresses or links contained in this book may have changed since publication and may no longer be valid. The views expressed in this work are solely those of the author and do not necessarily reflect the views of the publisher, and the publisher hereby disclaims any responsibility for them.

Any people depicted in stock imagery provided by Getty Images are models, and such images are being used for illustrative purposes only. Certain stock imagery © Getty Images.

Scripture taken from the New King James Version®. Copyright © 1982 by Thomas Nelson. Used by permission. All rights reserved.

ISBN: 978-1-6642-0164-4 (sc)
ISBN: 978-1-6642-0166-8 (hc)
ISBN: 978-1-6642-0165-1 (e)

Library of Congress Control Number: 2020914820

Print information available on the last page.

WestBow Press rev. date: 08/25/2020

ACKNOWLEDGMENTS

This book is dedicated to my wife, Sania Dookie, and children Raziela and Mikael Dookie, who have been a tower of strength and support over the years. They have supported me with their prayers, love, and constant encouragement. I want to especially thank my wife, Sania Dookie, who patiently and compassionately provided support and inspiration, which gave me the strength to achieve this milestone.

I would also like to thank Derek and Angela Maxson for their support in making my journey successful.

STRUCTURE OF THIS BOOK

There are three sections to this book. Section one will explore how God designed the mind and the role of healthy relationships in the developmental process. This will take into account the impact of early relationships between children and their primary attachment figures. This includes, a relationship with God and the primary caregiver. The second section will focus on what went wrong with God's design, the neurological impacts of psychological distress. Section three will explore God's plan to restore and heal the brain and its implication on improving the mind. I will explore how biblical meditation can facilitate healing of the mind of individuals who have experienced developmental trauma and its family members of depression and anxiety (Dookie, 2017).

In chapter two, there will be an exploration of what the mind is and how it is designed. In chapter three, I will look at the parent-child relationship and its impact on brain development. In chapter four, I will examine insecure attachment and how it affects the mind. Chapter five: investigating God, devotion, and the mind. Chapter six: God and neuroplasticity. Chapter seven: establishing biblical meditation. Chapter eight: healing the brain and the mind through biblical meditation from psychological distress caused by developmental trauma.

Chapter nine: biblical meditation and the healing of the physical faculty (brain). Chapter ten: biblical meditation and the healing of the psychological faculty. Chapter eleven: biblical meditation and the healing of the relational faculty. Chapter twelve: biblical meditation and the healing of the spiritual faculty. In Chapter thirteen, I will present sample outlines to facilitate one version of biblical reflection.

CONTENTS

SECTION ONE: GOD'S DESIGN

Stacey is a 23-year old young lady who has been suffering from low self-esteem, depression and severe anxiety for most of her life. Her coping mechanism was to use substances to calm the pangs of her anxiety and depression and to have more confidence in herself. She said, "I have tried everything, but nothing seemed to work."

Kevin was diagnosed with substance use disorders. He was sexually abused as a child and neglected by his primary attachment figures.

Stephanie was sexually abused at the age of twelve, raped again at age sixteen, and at age eighteen she got pregnant by a man who abused her physically and emotionally.

Patricia has suffered from chronic depression for the last two years.

Paul has constant nightmares and flashbacks about his experience growing up in South Africa.

Keisha's dad was an alcoholic who used to get drunk and physically and emotionally abuse her mom, her, and her sister.

It is no doubt that the individuals in the above vignettes have been through deep biopsychosocial-spiritual trauma which can severely impact their belief system and interpretation of their existence and alter their physiology. In this book, I will explore the impact these experiences specifically can have on the brain and the mind. I will discuss God's role in the healing and restoration of the mind from the effects of psychological distress. Psychological distress stemming from life's journey can lead to profoundly wounded pains that can derail one's life to the point of death, that is, physical, relational, psychological and spiritual death. You may know someone, or you may have experienced or are currently experiencing psychological distress. We all come from different walks of life and our individual journeys are different; however, there are common threads that run through all our stories. We can somehow relate to and empathize with each other.

In Canada, one in every four Canadians will experience mental illness or addiction in any given year. The United States statistics indicate that one in five Americans will experience mental illness each year. The implication of this reality is that mental disorders impact everyone. Research shows that 75% of mental illness challenges originated during childhood or adolescence. Early childhood experiences can have long-lasting implications throughout a lifespan. As we explore this further, be encouraged that it does not matter at what stage of our lives we are impacted by psychological distress; God can heal and restore that essence of our being (Dookie, 2017; Substance abuse and mental health services administration, 2015; Canadian Mental Health Association, 2016).

It is essential to make it clear that although we see tremendous benefits from the field of contemplative neuroscience, we must confess that we are only just scratching the surface. There is more to be learned about the mind than we already know. It is with humility and a sense of curiosity that we approach the subject of contemplative neuroscience, especially from the perspective that I am seeking to develop, that is, using a biblical model of meditative practice to facilitate changes in the brain. We know from research and practice that all activity we experience, whether we are actively or passively a part of it, leads to changes in the brain. This is the beauty of how God created the human mind. He created it in such a way that we can be attuned to every fiber of our existence and experience, interpreting and living life to the fullness of what He intended it to be. God's design of you was intentional. I now invite you to join me on this journey to explore attachment, psychopathology, neuroscience and their interconnections to God.

CHAPTER 1

THE MIND: GOD'S DESIGN

What is the Mind?

The mind has been one of the most discussed subjects in psychology and theology over the years. Suffice it to say, with all the grandiloquence of scholars in both theology and psychology today, we are still grappling to codify an acceptable definition of the mind. Most of what is proposed to be a definition of the mind are mainly components or functions of the brain. The mind is often conceptualized to be the amalgamation of cognitive faculties. These faculties are memory, thinking, perception, judgment, conscience, and consciousness. There are five fundamental aspects of the mind: spiritual, physical, psychological, relational, and subjective experiences. One researcher who has taken a bold step to define the mind is Dr. Daniel Siegel, a clinical professor of psychiatry at the UCLA School of Medicine. In his definition, he postulated that "the mind is an embodied and relational process that regulates the flow of energy and information" (Siegel, 2011).

The definition seemed to encapsulate both the thinking process of psychology and theology. There are four primary components of this description: embodiment, relational process, regulation, and the flow of energy and information.

Each of these ideas will be discussed from a Christo-theological perspective. Let's start with the phrase "flow of energy and information." In this regard, energy is not to be misunderstood as some mystical force

1

or superstitious phenomenon. In physics, energy is defined as the ability to do work. It is derived from the Greek word "energeia" which means "activity" or "operation." There are numerous types of energy: kinetic, potential, mechanical, electric, magnetic, gravitational, ionization, nuclear, elastic, sound wave, and thermal energy, just to name a few. The types of energy that are pertinent to our purpose are kinetic, electric, and chemical. Kinetic energy refers to the energy the body possesses due to its ability to be in motion. Chemical bonds relate to the energy within chemical bonds. Electrical energy is the energy stored in charged particles within an electric field. Chemical and electric energy play a crucial role in the movement of neurotransmitters between neurons in the brain (Siegel, 2011).

The term "embodied" often refers to the entire nervous system. The human body is very well-designed. There is the central nervous system with a spinal cord running from the brain to the body. Then, there is the peripheral nervous system in which the nerves run from the central nervous system to the extremities of the body. The peripheral nervous system is divided into two parts: the somatic nervous system and the autonomic nervous system. The autonomic nervous system regulates the following processes and body organs: blood pressure, breathing rate, stomach, liver, kidney, bladder, genitals, lungs, pupils, heart, sweat, digestive glands, and intestine. This embodiment points to the human body as designed by God. One aspect of the body, the brain, will be discussed in a later chapter.

What I would like you to keep in mind at this juncture is that this embodiment points to the intimate relationship between the mind and the body. God designed the mind and the body to function as one unit. All these systems lead to the links that are in the body-connections that are vital to the mind. Energy is the drive behind the functionality of all the body systems. The various organs of the body communicate with each other via the dispersion of energy. The content of this communication is essential to the way the body functions (Siegel, 2011; Dookie, 2017).

The third component of the above definition is the relational process. We are created to be in relationships. Thus, an explanation of the mind must include delineation of the importance of relationships. Consider the ten promises in Exodus, chapter twenty. The first four pertain to our relationship with God and the last six concern our relationships with each other. Jesus echoed this principle in the Book of Luke when He declared, "Love the Lord your God with all your heart and with all your soul and with all your strength and with all your mind and love your neighbor as yourself." From this, we can deduce that the relationship between God and humans and the relationship between humans

and humans are a vital part of what it means to be human. In both the divine-human and human-human relationship there is the movement of energy. This flow of energy is comprised of communicational contents. The content of this communication is the foundation to our relationship with God and our relationship with each other (Dookie, 2017; Siegel, 2011).

The final aspect of the above definition is regulatory. The regulatory process of the mind functions to observe and modify. The Bible states by beholding Jesus Christ we are changed into His image. As we spend time in a relationship with Jesus Christ and we learn to observe His love, compassion, care, patience, and kindness. We too are modified to become more loving, compassionate, caring, patient and kind. The Christian life desires to have the mind of Christ, to be like Christ. The word observe brings another vital concept to focus: awareness. Awareness points to one's ability to bring into focus the present moment. The awareness of Jesus in the present moment allows us to be able to approach life with love, compassion, care, patience and kindness towards self and others (Siegel, 2011; Dookie, 2017).

God's Design of the Mind

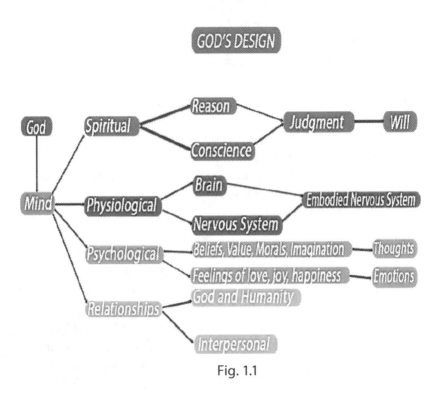

Fig. 1.1

God created us with a balanced mind. The components of our minds were equally proportioned in its operations, purposes, and processes. Our minds were designed perfectly. God created humanity perfectly upright and with a balanced mind. The magnitude and the potency of the various faculties of the mind are entirely developed. Every quality of the mind is well proportioned, each having a unique function. At the same time, each faculty depends upon the others for useful functionality. While the mind is designed for each faculty to have specialized features, it is also true that these specialized functions work together as an integrated whole. The integration of specialized functions is what makes the mind a masterpiece of God's creation. Similarly,

when I discuss the physical faculty (brain), you will recognize that the brain has different parts with specialized functions, but these different areas of the brain integrate their specialized tasks in order for the brain to function optimally.

There are four components of the mind: spiritual, physical, psychological, and relational. The mind governs the whole person: all our actions, good or bad, have their birthplace in the mind. God designed our minds to dwell on things that are pure, holy, righteous, perfect, and eternal. The brain monitors and regulates all our actions. The figures below are used to depict the different components of the mind. Let's consider each faculty of the mind and see how God designed it.

Spiritual Faculty of the Mind

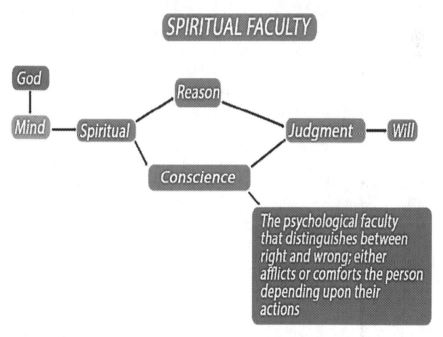

Fig. 1.2

In the mind, God designed the spiritual faculty of the mind with two components: reason and conscience. We are created to use logic and conscience to make a judgment. It is our ability to make the decision that expresses our free will. Reason points our capacity to approach God from our own intrinsic choice conscientiously. The reality is that God intended that we worship Him out of love and free choice. In other words, "reason" being a part of the spiritual faculty suggests that worship is a reasonable endeavor. In addition to reason, we have a conscience. The Greek word for conscience is defined as the psychological faculty that enables us to distinguish between right and wrong.

In the book of Genesis, the Bible stated that Eve was deceived. In deceiving Eve, Satan reasoned with her, thus causing her conscience to become clouded.

Therefore, she chose to eat the fruit. A closer look at the exchange between Eve and Satan illustrates that the root of the discussion was about worship. Satan told the woman that if she ate the fruit, she would become like God, knowing good and evil. This desire of the woman to be like God is the root of self-worship and the cause for spiritual separation from God and spiritual degeneration. The source of self-worship is of the devil and this was and is still a tool used to chisel away at God's perfect creation of the mind. This evil impact is imperative to understand; it helps us to see our need of God and why we need Him to restore our minds.

In the next chapter, I will discuss the impact of sin on the mind. Reason and conscience are two faculties that God gave to us to distinguished us from animals. These faculties allow us to have open access to God. This is the privilege that Adam and Eve were given-the ability to have unhindered access and communication with God. Now that we have looked at the spiritual faculty of the mind, I will now address the physical faculty of the mind.

Reason and the Mind

Consider the following verse from Romans 12:1-2: "I beseech you, therefore, brethren, by the mercies of God, that you present your bodies a living sacrifice, holy, acceptable to God, which is your reasonable service." This verse is a call to worship and pay keen attention; Paul refers to worship as reasonable service.

In Isaiah 1:18, God called his people to come and reason with Him, and again in 1 Peter 3:15: "But sanctify the Lord God in your hearts; and always be ready to give an answer to everyone who asks you a reason concerning the hope that is in you, with humility and fear:" Note that Peter indicated that we are supposed to be able to reason out our faith.

That is, in worshiping God, we should be ready to logically explain our rationale for praising God.

Conscience and the Mind

The word conscience is used approximately 31 times in the Bible. In Paul's epistle, conscience is used primarily concerning the making of judgment. The aptitude to choose between wrong and right is modulated by the conscience. The next time you are faced with a situation that determines a wrong or right answer, remember it is your conscience that is at work. The conscience is the faculty of the spiritual organ that establishes obedience as a moral requirement. Based on the scriptures, God designed the conscience for three fundamental functions.

The first purpose of the conscience is to bear witness. In Romans 2:15, the apostle stated that the conscience bears witness. God designed the conscience to attest to the realities of our lives; in other words, the conscience stands as a witness to the genuineness of our lives. The second function is introspection, that is, we use our conscience to evaluate our own lives.

In Acts 24:16, Luke stated, "so I strive always to keep my conscience clear before God and all people." Again in 1 Corinthians 4:4, the apostle said, "My conscience is clear, but that does not make me innocent, it is the Lord who judges me." These two verses illustrate the fact that we use the conscience to examine our lives. Paul said that his conscience was clear, meaning when he investigated his life, as far as he could tell his conscience set him free. The third function of the conscience is to undergird our value system. Our values system should be based on the Bible, which consists of instructions from God on how we are to live. When we have a good, moral, and godly base to inform our conscience, then our value system will automatically be permeated with righteousness and fastened into the restorative and maintaining power of God.

When our ethical, moral, and philosophical life principles are to be anchored in the word of God, we begin to possess a balanced and healthy function of the conscience. The three functions of the conscience, witness-bearing, introspection, and value system are integral to a healthy mind. When our conscience and reason play a role in the manner in which God designed it, then the judgments that we make will be in tune with the will of God for our life; this is how God intended it to be. In the next segment, I will explore the brain structures that God designed to function with both reason and conscience.

Physical Faculty of the Mind

When referring to the physical structure of the mind, I am primarily thinking of the brain; however, the entire body is essential to proper functioning of the mind. For the purpose of this book, the emphasis will be on specific areas of the cortical and subcortical brain structures.

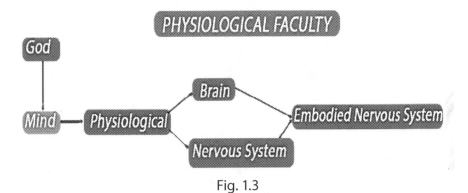

Fig. 1.3

The subcortical areas include the reticular formation (arousal, alertness, and wakefulness), amygdala (detects, learns about, and responds to stimuli), basal ganglia (refines movement and modulates the motivation for movement), insula (process feelings associated with risk, gut-feeling, uncertainty, personal agency, and sense of self), hypothalamus (regulation of eating, drinking, mating, endocrine system, and autonomic nervous system), ventral striatum and nucleus accumbens (rewards centre),

and ventral tegmental area (manufactures and releases dopamine) (Andrew & Iversen, 2003; Tang Y.-Y., et al., 2010).

The cortical structures include the prefrontal cortex (Executive), orbitofrontal cortex (store and process rewards in the environment), ventromedial prefrontal cortex (evaluate unlearned emotions), dorsolateral prefrontal cortex (evaluate learned emotions), and the anterior cingulate cortex (Monitor brain) (Sullivan, The neurobiology of attactment to nurturing and abusive caregivers, 2012). These brain areas in the subcortical and cortical regions have been elaborated on in chapter two.

The brain is the faculty of the mind that controls the entire body. It is the brain that modulates the whole body. The other organs and systems of the body depend on the brain. Thus, a healthy brain will result in a healthy body. The enfeeblement of the physical faculty will significantly impair the mind from making effective decisions or the ability to choose between right and wrong. Consider the brain to be the central processing unit of our bodies.

Psychological Faculty of the Mind

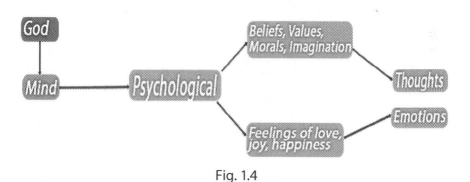

Fig. 1.4

The third faculty of the mind is the psychological faculty. There are two components of the psychological faculty: our thoughts and our emotions. The Bible stated that the way in which we think determines who we are (Proverbs 23:7). Our thoughts are influenced by our beliefs, our values, our morals and our imagination. There are two types of thoughts: automatic and constructive. Automatic thoughts are those thoughts that come without our influence; on the other hand, constructive ideas are those thoughts that we deliberately engage with in our minds. Our thoughts are essential to our habits, and our habits form character, that is, who we are on the basic level. God in His wisdom saw it fit to entrust us with a mind that is governed by free will. As a faculty of the mind, the psychological dimension of the mind must be fed with pure thoughts, positive thoughts and elevating thoughts. This cultivation must be deliberate, our thoughts must be permeated with the love, joy, hope, peace, and the will of Christ; this will, in turn, influence our beliefs.

The beliefs we have about God, ourselves, others and the world around us will profoundly influence our thinking patterns. If we have good thoughts about God, self, others and the world, we will enjoy peak psychological health. The basic meaning of "belief" is the acceptance of something or someone to be true. Maybe you are familiar with the saying that "belief kills and belief cures." What are your beliefs about God? Do you believe that He loves and cares for you? Do you believe that Jesus died to set you free from the power of sin? Do you believe that God works all things for our good?

The beliefs we have of our God, ourselves, others and the world we live in will influence our values and our morals. The family values we adapt to in our homes will be influenced by our beliefs. It is our responsibility to control our thoughts and our imaginations. If the imagination is impure, that mind will be riddled with sickness and poor psychological health. The Bible encourages us to bring all our thoughts and ideas into captivity to the obedience of Jesus Christ. In psychology, we have a principle known as mastery beliefs. This concept is predicated on the individual ability to perceive control.

When a person with a firm conviction that he/she has the power to attain a desirable positive outcome and prevent an aversive result, this is referred to as master belief. Master belief is something that God has given to us, and we can know that God will work out our eternal outcome to His desire and prevent any harm that may seek to avert our eternal salvation.

The second component of the psychological faculty is the emotions. What is an emotion? Emotions can be described as multidimensional. Emotion is a subjective, biological, purposive and expressive phenomenon (Mauss et al., 2005). It is that which determines the way we feel, such as, anger, sadness, love, joy, happiness and guilt. It is biological because it prepares a body to respond to the specific feelings that are experienced in a given moment or period. It has a purpose because it prepares us for action. These actions are influenced by urges and impulse. Finally, it is expressive. When we experience certain emotions, we exude certain recognizable facial expressions, posture and vocal signals. There are different types of emotions: joy, sadness, love, anger, fear, disgust, interest, pride, contempt, shame and guilt. It is my conviction that God did not create us to experience negative emotions such as guilt, shame, sadness, anger, and fear. These feelings came into our psychological make up as a result of sin. Note, it is not a sin to experience these emotions; these emotions give us information that something is not right. The impact of wrongdoing on the four faculties will be discussed in proceeding chapters.

Relational Faculty of the Mind

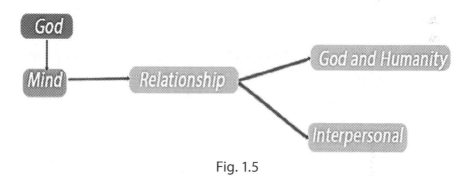

Fig. 1.5

The final faculty of the mind is the relational faculty. This faculty is summarized in Jesus' definition of the Law. Jesus indicated that the fulfillment of the Law is to love the Lord our God with all our strength and with all our soul and our neighbor as ourselves. Notice in the law of the mind as it pertains to a relationship, we are called into a loving relationship with God and then called to extend this love to neighbors. The relational faculty has two components: there is the vertical component, our relationship with God, and there is a horizontal component, our interpersonal connections with each other. Even the ten commandments are divided into these two parts; the first four point to our relationship with God, and the last six points to our relationships with each other.

This chapter explored the definition of the mind, and how God designed the mind. The mind has four faculties: the spiritual, physiological, psychological, and the interpersonal. God created humanity with a perfectly balanced mind.

In acknowledgment of God and His grand design, all true knowledge and real development have their source as depicted in the above image. It does not matter where we turn; in the spiritual, physical, mental, or relational realm, in whatever we behold, apart from the blight of sin, this knowledge is revealed. Whatever line of investigation we pursue, with a sincere purpose to arrive at truth, we are brought in touch with the unseen, mighty Intelligence that is working in and through all. The mind of humans is brought into communion with the mind of God-the finite with the Infinite. The effect of such communion on body and mind and soul is beyond estimate.

In the next chapter, I will examine the physiological faculty through the prism of the relational faculty. For the purpose of this book, the physiological faculty is the brain. I will first explore brain development through healthy relationships with primary caregivers.

CHAPTER 2

PARENT-CHILD RELATIONSHIPS

The science of cultivating the mind is the highest responsibility given to humanity. When a child is born into the world, the parents are given the divine responsibility to nurture, care, and strengthen the young mind from birth to adulthood. The mind is to be trained in such a manner that all four faculties are guided by the impulse of the heart of God.

The moment we are conceived in our mother's womb, the journey of connections begins. The prenatal stage is the primary starting point of where attachment germinates. There is research linking a mother's mental state to the psychological distress that a child may experience post-natal. The fetus is susceptible to the mother's experiences while he or she is developing. The baby continually receives incoming messages from mom. While the placenta is protective, there is research that indicates chemical signals from a mother's mental state could cross over into the placenta. Thus, if the mother is depressed or anxious, this will influence how the child's brain develops both prenatal and postnatal. What this means is that the environment in which we developed has a lot to do with our course in life. Notice, the first environment is our mother's womb. Let me clarify; this is not an indication of blaming mothers for what might or might not have happened to their children. The fact of the matter is that mothers also find themselves in uncertain environments in which their psychological states become disconnected.

Many children are born into homes that are not nurturing or with parents and primary attachment figures who are not equipped to provide a nurturing environment. When this happens, the children are predisposed to experience negative interpersonal connections. These early relationships form the bases of how children develop. In the work of John Bowlby and Mary Ainsworth, they studied the interpersonal relationship between primary attachment figures and children. They formed a field of attachment theory. In their work, they highlighted four types of attachment styles: secure, insecure, anxious-avoidant, and anxious-resistance. These attachment styles signify an organized pattern of emotions, behaviors, and expectations that individuals have for how others will respond in relationships (Ainsworth & Bowlby, 1991; Azari, et al., Neural correlates of religious experience, 2001; Dookie, 2017).

Secure Attachment

In the work of Bowlby and Ainsworth, they developed the theory of attachment. A vital part of attachment theory that is directly connected to the healthy development of the spiritual, physical, psychological and relational faculty is a secure attachment. Secure attachment is underpinned by the healthy relationships between child and primary attachment figures. We are securely attached when we feel confident about the availability of our primary attachment figures to meet our needs. Children who are brought up in a nurturing environment are less predisposed to biopsychosocial challenges.

They perform better in school and in the community. This does not mean homes without flaws exist; rather, there are homes in which the following characteristics are evident: love, forgiveness, hope, kindness, compassion, unconditional positive regards, and genuine care (Davidson & Lutz, 2008; Davidson R., 2008). Often, there needs to be only one primary attachment figure who seeks to create a nurturing environment, and this will make an enormous difference in the lives of the children. Before moving on to the other attachment styles, the question of how to develop secure attachment will be addressed.

Attachment relationship is developed between the parent and the child or primary attachment figure. Attachment relationship is symbiotic, in that, it functions to down-regulate the stress that both the child and the primary attachment figure experience. This relationship creates the platform in which the primary attachment figure tunes into their own emotional world and the emotional world of their children. Secure attachment is developed when parents are sensitive to the internal world or internal working model of their children, and this allows the children to become integrated bio psychosocially.

In other words, the person who we become is pivotally dependent on the context of relationships. It is through a secure attachment that we learn to love, care, and have the ability to empathize with others. The Bible talks about having a perfect and good conscience (1 Peter 3:16; 1 Timothy 1:19; Acts 23:1:). Attune attachment bonding is the source of perfect and good conscience. If children are to develop a healthy morality of conscience, then it is crucial for them to be in healthy relationships.

I want to you consider what it would mean to have a securely attached relationship with God. This is a topic that I will explore in the last section of this chapter; however, at this juncture, what I want you to do is to consider the development of the brain through secure attachment to God. If our children are given a real Christian environment of love, compassion, genuine care, and the opportunity to learn about God's plan for their lives, just imagine the impact of a God-centered home on the various parts of the brain that will be briefly explored in the chapter.

Secure Attachment and Brain Development

A secure attachment has a profound impact on brain development. In safe bonding relationships, children form neuronal pathways that promote an ability to cultivate long-lasting, healthy relationships. Genetics and environment are the two chief executive officers of brain development. Our brain development is continuously changing as a result of interactions between genes and environment. Go on a journey with me to see how our brain develops.

First, it begins a as neural tube. At this stage cells are being born, initiating the process of neurogenesis. Secondly, these cells then travel to their ultimate destination in the brain, a process known as migration. The collection of cells forms branches; some are referred to as axons for inputs, and others are referred to as dendrites for outputs. The axons and dendrites are called neurons. The average human brain has 100 billion neurons. The collection of these neurons forms pathways and circuits in the brain. The neurons communicate with each other via electrical-chemical interactions between neurons. The gaps between neurons are called synapses (van der Kolk, Developmental trauma disorder: A new, rational diagnosis for children with complex trauma histories, 2008; Yyrka, et al., 2013).

The process of neurogenesis and migration takes place in the prenatal stage of brain development. Neuronal pathways and circuits develop at a rapid pace during the first seven years of life, especially the initial three years. As was mentioned before, it is at this stage that the delicate balance between genes and environment starts to interchange on a consistent basis. It is during these formative years that the process of "experience-dependent plasticity" is super active. What a child learns in these early years will form circuits and pathways in the brain that can impact their output in later life. In the first twelve years of growth, a child has more neurons than he or she needs, thus the brain goes to neuronal pruning. It is like pruning a tree so that it produces more and at a higher efficacy. In secure relationships, a child's mind is organized for success and resilience.

Resilience suggests that even though these children may face challenges in their lives, they deal with them effectively because of their early positive relationships with a primary attachment figure (Van der Kolk & Pynoos, 2009; Siegel, 2011).

In a secure attachment relationship, the different areas of the brain are at an advantage by being properly developed. There are three areas of the brain that are pertinent to efficient functioning: the brain stem, the limbic system, and the cortical brain structures. The brainstem consists of three main parts: the medulla, pons, and midbrain. The brainstem regulates automatic or essential functions. For instance, the medulla functions to control breathing, swallowing, blood pressure, and heart rate. The pons serves to connect the cerebellum to the cerebrum, and the midbrain controls basic vision and hearing. These functions are essential for survival. Thus, from a developmental perspective, these brain areas mature more efficiently in a safe and loving environment (van der Kolk, The neurobiolology of childhood trauma and abuse, 2003; Sperry, 2016).

The brainstem functions on the bases of rhythm, like the rhythm of breathing, heart rate, and blood pressure. A key enhancer of effective rhythm in humans is relationships. Our brains respond to various rhythms in our environment: the rhythm of voice, touch, sounds, and tunes. In other words, secure attachment strengthens brainstem connections because it embodies the primary attachment figures using their voice to soothe the child, their touches

to care for the child and reassuring sounds to calm the child. The reality is that we interact with rhythm when we engage in conversations. We use our hands, faces, and our entire body, thus children synchronize and regulate their bodies to the way they read our body language. For instance, with both my children, whenever they are dysregulated, if I hold them to my chest and they start to listen to my heart rate, they tend to settle down and regain homeostasis. This phenomenon is due to the fact that they begin to regulate their rhythm to mine; hence, it aids in calming them down (Coutois & Ford, 2013; Debbane, et al., 2016).

The limbic area is impacted positively by an environment that is nurturing and loving. The limbic system is often referred to as our emotional brain because it is integral to the function of emotions. The limbic system can be classified into two sections: the subcortical structures and the portions of the cerebral cortex. Areas of the cortical regions that are in the limbic system are hippocampus, insular cortex, and orbital frontal cortex. The subcortical areas of the limbic system are hypothalamus, thalamus, and amygdala. Though there are other areas of the brain that are associated with the limbic system, those mentioned above are pertinent to understanding regulation and rhythm, nurture and environment (Gabowitz, Zucker, & Cook, 2008).

Hippocampus

The hippocampus is vital for explicit memory. This type of memory requires conscious thoughts, for instance, what I had for lunch today or naming animals that live in North America. In other words, explicit memory deals with facts. The hippocampus in children who are at the age to learn a language is more active. Research has demonstrated that children in homes that are loving and caring tend to speak at an earlier stage than children within a negative environment. The hippocampus is essential for conscious awareness and memory retrieval. Children who are in a safe environment will perform better in school because their hippocampus is at its best. One way to think of the hippocampus is to use the suffix "campus" which has to do with a university campus or a place of learning. Children in secure attachment interpersonal relationships will excel in all areas of learning. The hippocampus also attaches salience to emotional memory, that is, memories that are created by being connected to emotional stimuli will be able to be recalled more readily (Hogue, 2014; Lewis-Fernandez, Das, Alfonso, Weissman, & Olfson, 2005).

Insula Cortex

The insula cortex serves to monitor the body's internal state. It is that area of the brain that allows us to say, "I have a gut feeling." It is associated with feelings of risk, uncertainty, personal agency and the sense of self. Children who are in a safe interpersonal relationship will better judge situations that are risky and uncertain. They develop a healthier sense of self and are more confident in who they are as an individual, having a strong sense of individuality but also a strong sense of connectivity with others (McEwen, Nasca, & Gray, 2016).

Hypothalamus

Integration of behaviors, to a significant degree, is mediated by the hypothalamus. Integration is a topic that will be discussed in later chapters of this book. The hypothalamus is a master control on the regulation of the autonomic nervous system and the endocrine system. The autonomic nervous system is divided into two parts: the parasympathetic nervous system, and the sympathetic nervous system. Whenever a person becomes aroused, the sympathetic nervous system is activated. The parasympathetic nervous system works to counterbalance the sympathetic nervous system. Let's think about this from the perspective of chaos and calmness. A child in a securely attached relationship will be better able to calm the chaos in their lives more efficiently. This is partly due to the fact that the hypothalamus is better able to control the autonomic nervous system in children who are in a safe interpersonal relationship with their primary attachment figures. It is the hypothalamus that regulates the fight, flight, feeding, freezing, and mating phenomena (Nash & Newberg, 2013).

Thalamus

The grand central station of the brain is the thalamus. It receives and sends information to and from the cerebral cortex. The cerebral cortex will be discussed in the next section. The thalamus is associated with the regulation of consciousness, sleep, and alertness.

Researchers have suggested that children in a secure relationship have significantly more grey matter in the thalamus.

Amygdala

Think of the amygdala as the brain's alarm system. If something goes wrong as it relates to any emotional stimuli, the alarm is triggered. It aids our body to detect, learn about, and respond to environmental stimuli. This encompasses both threat-eliciting and reward-eliciting associations. A secure attachment plays a crucial role in preventing the amygdala from being triggered. There is research that indicates that when a caregiver's facial expressions are supportive, caring, attuned to, and engaging, the child experiences positive sentiment override; the child experiences more positive emotions than negative emotions. It also suggests that in the presence of harmful emotions, these children are better able to ride the tides of negative emotions (Van der Kolk & Pynoos, 2009). Children in a secure, attached interpersonal relationship show normal development of amygdala volume in comparison to those in insecurely attached relationships, a topic that will be discussed in the upcoming chapter.

Basal Ganglia, Ventral Striatum, Nucleus Accumbens, and the Ventral Tegmental Area

There are four areas not previously mentioned above that are crucial to the study and understanding of brain development and attachment.

These are the basal ganglia, ventral striatum, nucleus accumbens, and the ventral tegmental area. These areas of the brain are responsible for the manufacturing and releasing of dopamine. Secure attachment stimulates that basal ganglia to be more efficient in carrying out motivational modulation of movement and actions. If you recall, the section on the brain stem where I discussed rhythm as an essential part of the brain stem, is the basal ganglia, working in collaboration with the brain stem to bring about a motivational initiative to modulate our actions in the way we move our bodies. Hopefully, you see the importance of secure relationships, especially in early development (Sperry, 2016).

Individuals in secure interpersonal relationships will activate the brain's reward center, that is, the ventral striatum, nucleus accumbens, and the ventral tegmental area. The ventral tegmental area is ground zero for the manufacturing and dissemination of dopamine throughout the brain. Just imagine the place in your mind that causes you to experience pleasure. The pleasure of being content, happy, joyful, satisfied, and relaxed would be from your nucleus accumbens. It is the interconnected working relationship of these brain areas that are responsible for the production of and release of dopamine. Dopamine is the brain's feel-good neurotransmitter. Being in healthy relationships allow these areas of the brain to function at top capacity to bring joy into our lives.

We learn from our environment, the events, the encounters, the experiences, and if the circumstances, contacts, and experiences are positive, then these brain areas release dopamine, and we conclude that our environment is safe. A safe environment is a place where growth and development can take place. The motivation for success, the willpower to strive, and the determination to keep focus are all strengthened through positive, early interpersonal relationships. With the constant release of dopamine in a positive environment, we become accustomed to anticipating reward-related results. What we can conclude about the dopamine pathway- ventral striatum, nucleus accumbens and the ventral tegmental area is that it is one of the main starting points for positive emotions.

As we have seen so far, individuals in secure interpersonal relationships will develop a stronger emotional brain this leads to higher emotional intelligence and resilience. Emotional intelligence is pertinent to our daily lives. It is emotional intelligence that allows us to recognize our feelings and be able to identify feelings in others. Picture this in terms of brain development; children are better able to name their feelings and utilize their emotions to facilitate cognitive and behavioral responses in the secure attachment environment. A healthy limbic equals stronger emotional resilience; in other words, secure attachment helps us to develop strong emotional resilience, thus we can face negative stimuli in any environment with hope.

In the previous section, I briefly explored the impact of a secure attachment on the limbic system. In this portion, I will talk about secure attachment and the cerebral cortex. There are five primary areas of the cerebral cortex that I will touch on concerning a secure interpersonal relationship. These areas are prefrontal cortex, orbital prefrontal cortex, ventromedial prefrontal cortex, dorsolateral prefrontal cortex, and anterior cingulate cortex. Research has demonstrated that when we are nurtured in a loving-compassionate environment, our frontal lobe integrates in such a manner that we can have a more profound sense of empathy, flexibility, and interconnectedness. Let's consider the four areas of the cerebrum that are mentioned above, specifically highlighting their development through the lens of secure interpersonal relationships.

Prefrontal Cortex

The prefrontal cortex is responsible for executive functions. Executive functions can be divided into two segments, logical and emotional. You might be asking yourself, "executive function and emotion - can those two be merged?" Well, that is the reason why early secure attached relationships are so vital to development. Research postulated that secure attachment allows the prefrontal cortex to regulate the expression of emotions in an appropriate matter. Have you ever wondered why some people are better able to control their emotions more effective than others? A key reason most times lies in the environment in which that person grew up. Secure interpersonal relationships allow the prefrontal cortex to function at its full potential; thus, we are better able to make plans, to set goals, and to formulate intentions.If you want your children to be more efficient in making the right choice with pure intentions, it is crucial for you to create an environment in which we nurture the development of the prefrontal cortex.

The prefrontal cortex underpins motivational behaviors, in that it regulates emotions, executive functions, and personal striving. Recall from the previous section, I discussed the ventral striatum, nucleus accumbens and the ventral tegmental area as being ground zero for emotions. However, the prefrontal cortex also plays a crucial role in our experience of emotions. Children in safe interpersonal relationships will develop a thicker prefrontal cortex; in other words, there will be more grey matter in this part of the brain. This will make them better able to make plans, initiate plans, regulate emotions, formulate intentions, and strive more effectively.

Orbital Frontal Cortex

Have you ever wondered why some people choose one option over another or why some individuals prefer one thing over another? You may be thinking to yourself, "what do preferences and choices have to do with early interpersonal relationships?" We prefer or choose one option over the other based on reward-related information in the environment. The orbital frontal cortex is the brain area that allows us to have a preference or choice and to choose based on reward-related details on environmental objects.

A secure attachment will aid children in developing healthy neural connections in the orbital frontal cortex that will influence preferences.

The willpower to decide to do the right thing for the right reason is hinged off the development of a healthy orbital frontal cortex. Think about it: the power of early interpersonal connection can lead a child to develop a preference and willpower to choose correctly. In other words, inappropriate actions on the child's part can be significantly mitigated by a secure attachment. The orbital prefrontal cortex supplies the ability to be human; it allows people to have empathy, read signals from others, and retain autobiography information. This brain area thrives in an environment that is engaging and where a primary attachment figure is attuned to the child.

Ventromedial Prefrontal Cortex

The functions of the ventromedial prefrontal cortex are emotional control, appraising unlearned emotional values of sensory rewards, social flexibility, and internal body states. Research postulates that the following roles of the ventromedial prefrontal cortex include valuation, inhibition, and use of rules. The appraisal of unlearned emotion is crucial for the development of emotional resilience. As a child engages with his or her environment, he or she will encounter various feelings. It is their ventromedial prefrontal cortex that allows children to evaluate these feelings. In my own practice, I have often encountered adult clients who are not able to effectively assess their emotions. Often, I have had to teach them emotional vocabularies. Studies have indicated that children in healthy interpersonal environments will develop a thicker and more active ventromedial prefrontal cortex. More active means that it is firing more frequently, thus, these children are more apt to appraise emotions.

The ability to effectively evaluate emotions will give these individuals a better sense of understanding their internal states. They can better describe how they are feeling inside. Recall the section of the insula, in which the insula aids in the gut-feelings, such as disgust, shame, and guilt. The ventromedial prefrontal cortex works closely with the insula in informing us about our deep internal feelings.

Dorsolateral Prefrontal Cortex

Imagine the place in your brain where you store emotional meaning and value; the dorsolateral prefrontal cortex is that place. The environment in which we grew up fosters the way in which we learn emotions and the values we ascribe to emotional experiences. Children in a secure interpersonal relationship are at an advantage of learning appropriate emotional expression and the value of feelings. These types of emotional memories are stored in the dorsolateral prefrontal cortex. Thus, when making decisions, we retrieve this stored environmental information from the dorsolateral prefrontal cortex to create an emotionally informed choice.

Dr. Courtney Dookie

There are two other essential functions of the dorsolateral prefrontal cortex. These are, the power to resist temptation, and the willingness to be selfless, that is, not acting selfishly. Think about your child or yourself delaying immediate gratification for long-term goals. The dorsolateral prefrontal cortex aids humans with the willpower to override temptation or urges. As was mentioned before, the dorsolateral prefrontal cortex has a vital inhibitory role in decision making. Thirdly, think of your child deciding to share their toys during play rather than keeping his/her toys for themselves. This ability to act selflessly in social interaction is a function of the dorsolateral prefrontal cortex.

Research indicates that children in a securely attached relationship have a thicker grey matter in the dorsolateral prefrontal cortex and their dorsolateral prefrontal cortex remains more active. Notice that emotional intelligence and social graces, such as justice, equality, equity, care, and empathy, can all be traced to the dorsolateral prefrontal cortex. This is another critical reason children need a caring, nurturing, and supportive environment.

Anterior Cingulate Cortex

Kevin needs to decide if he is going to drink water or pop. He enjoys the sugary taste of soda, but he is aware that water is better for his health. Kevin will have to make a judgment call. The part of the brain that aids in his judgment call is the anterior cingulate cortex.

The anterior cingulate cortex functions in deciding what gets attention, monitoring conflicts, making choices, and making decisions. In the analogy above, Kevin has to determine the long-term consequences of drinking water or pop. In other words, he needs to be able to predict consequences of his actions. Maybe if Kevin has a strong desire for soda, the anterior cingulate cortex will alert other brain areas to the need for increased cognitive control to resolve the conflicts. In doing so, Kevin learns to regulate himself.

The ability to manage conflict effectively is the work of the anterior cingulate cortex. When there is a conflict, the anterior cingulate allocates cognitive recourses. These resources include attention and decision making in a way that the outcome addresses the desired goals. Secure interpersonal relationships strengthen neuronal connections in the anterior cingulate cortex. Numerous researchers indicate that children in secure attachment relationships have better cerebral blood flow in the anterior cingulate cortex. This enables these individuals to make better decisions and make more efficient judgment calls. The data shows that children in stable home environments make safer choices during their lives, even in their youthful years.

Throughout this chapter, I have highlighted different brain areas and how healthy relationships impact these areas. I want you to know that even though we can differentiate brain areas and their functions, the brain does not function differentiated. It serves as an integrated whole.

SECTION TWO:
WHAT WENT WRONG?

The entrance of sin into the human family broke our relationship with God and each other. God created us to have an intimate connection with Himself and each other. We were built to have fellowship with God and sin destroyed that relationship. If you recall from Genesis, when sin entered, Adam and Eve's relationship with each other was also broken. They became selfish, self-focused, and self-conscious. In response to the above question, what went wrong? Sin is what is wrong because at its core it is a broken relationship. The fact that our relationship with God and with each other has been broken became a generational disease. Thus, parents who are supposed to be loving, caring, nurturing and affectionate to their children are instead in some cases aggressive, unloving, neglectful and without compassion to their children, this then leads to what John Bowlby and colleagues referred to as an insecure attachment. The following chapter will examine insecure attachment and its impact on the physiological faculty (the brain).

CHAPTER 3

WHAT WENT WRONG?

The image below provides a summary of the effects of insecure attachment on all the faculties of the mind.

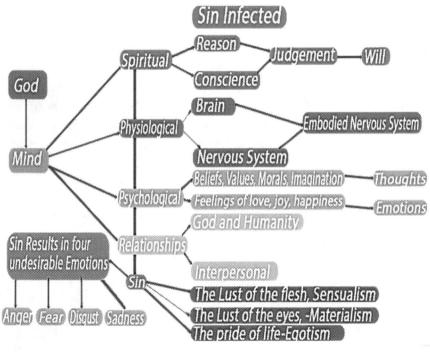

Fig. 1.6

The plan that God intended for humanity through the development of the mind was thwarted by sin. Parents who are supposed to take care of their children find themselves in a situation where they are either incapable of caring or choose not to care because they themselves were never nurtured. In light of this, the four faculties of the mind were severely damaged. The root of this damage is illustrated through the scientific theory developed by John Bowlby and company known as the attachment theory. The aspect of the attachment theory that is directly related to the development of a chaotic or a rigid mind is insecure attachment. Insecure attachment negatively influences all four faculties of the brain. An insecure attachment stems from homes/ environments that are primarily negative. Primary attachment figures in these homes are not attuned with their children's needs. They are often insensitive, and the children experience persistent and consistent rejections. Children who grew up in such toxic homes are predisposed to develop mental illnesses such as depression, anxiety, personality disorders, developmental trauma disorders, substance use disorders, and interpersonal difficulties.

There are direct correlations between brain development and attachment figures. The environment where children develop can empower or disempower those children. Children develop bonds with their primary attachment figures; these bonds determine to a large degree the brain development of children. John Bowlby and his colleagues developed the attachment theory to explain the primary attachment figure-child relationship. Based on Bowlby's research, an attachment is a unique relationship between an infant and their primary attachment figures; this relationship underpins healthy development or unhealthy development. It is an intrinsic bio-psycho-social and spiritual reaction of the child within the environment. This response is fundamental to the child/children in facilitating their basic needs.

The relationship between a child and his or her primary attachment figure is so fundamental that research has demonstrated that the interactions between genetics and childhood experience can change the structure and functions of the brain. The brain of a child who grows up in a stable, nurturing environment will adapt to environmental changes in a healthy manner. The attachment relationship is an essential component to the developing brain, as was discussed in chapter two.

Insecure attachment, on the other hand, is associated with lack of affection and unhealthy social interactions, which will halt the physical development of the brain. A child's brain is wired to form an attachment to primary and secondary attachment figures. The brain's attachment circuitry fires based on the interaction between the child and their principal figures. This circuitry changes as the child learns about the primary attachment figures and their roles. Insecure attachment develops in an environment that is void of a nurturing primary attachment figure. Such an environment is traumatic for children. These children suffer from emotional disturbances, social impairment, attention difficulties, and cognitive challenges and are more hostile and aggressive. The impact of insecure attachment will inevitably damage the brain-the result is often seen in adulthood, through substance use, multiple psychiatric disorders, and social impairments.

Neurological Impact of Insecure Attachment

In discussing the neurological implications of an insecure attachment, it is essential to address how the brain develops and how, as children continue to grow, their brains experience change in both structures and functions. The brain's development begins in the uterus and continues after birth. In the first five years of life, grey and white matter expands in volume. At ages 7-17, the white matter continues to expand. The size of the corpus callosum, hippocampus, frontal cortex, and amygdala increase throughout development (Singleton, et al., 2014).

Insecure Attachment and the Amygdala

An insecure attachment slows or halts the progress of these brain areas. Research has demonstrated that insecure attachment is directly linked to increased amygdala reactivity. Think of the amygdala as the brain's alarm system; when it is triggered, the body experiences distress. Picture a home in which the alarm is triggered but never turned off. This is reminiscent of what is happening in our bodies when the amygdala is triggered. The amygdala is central in activating the hypothalamic-pituitary-adrenal (HPA) axis. The HPA-axis mediates the stress response of the body. An insecure attachment reduces the size of the hippocampus, and the amygdala becomes hyper-responsive. This leads to an overstimulation of the noradrenergic system and a decreased volume of the frontal cortex. A part of the frontal cortex is the prefrontal cortex which consists of the anterior cingulate cortex (ACC) and the medial frontal gyrus, which functions to inhibit stress responses and emotional reactivity due to amygdala trigger. These areas of the brain are responsible for learning, memory, and effective regulation (Dookie, 2017).

So, imagine a child who is always being triggered by the environment; it would be difficult for that child to focus in school to learn. The child will have challenges in regulating their emotions. Given that the child has difficulty learning and managing emotions, what ends up happening most of the time is the child begins to "act out." The reality is the child is coping in the best way he/she knows how. Often these children are diagnosed with ADHD, ADD, or other behavioral problems. These behavioral problems can continue into adulthood, where adults act out in different ways: some use substances, and some engage in unhealthy behaviors, such as gambling, pornography, etc.

Insecure Attachment and Dendrites

Research indicates that individuals who experienced trauma have significant shrinkage in the hippocampal dendrites and dentate gyrus neurons. The dentate gyrus neurons and the hippocampus are necessary for memory consolidation, storage, and retrieval. Developmental trauma, which is the source of insecure attachment, leads to long-term neuroadaptive changes in the ventral tegmental area of the dopamine neurons. The ventral tegmental is responsible for dopamine production, and dopamine is the feel-good neurotransmitter. In other words, individuals with an insecure attachment will find it difficult to enjoy the pleasures of life. Insecure attachment negatively impairs brain structures, neural circuits, neurotransmitters systems, and neuropeptides. It impacts brain stem, limbic system, and cortical brain structures (Dookie, 2017; van der Kolk, Developmental trauma disorder: A new, rational diagnosis for children with complex trauma histories, 2008). In other words, an insecure attachment affects the entire brain negatively.

An insecure attachment reduces dendritic spins and grey matter in the brain. Dendritic spins are encompassing neurotransmitter receptors and organelles. The spins function as a signaling system that is fundamental for synaptic functions and plasticity. Synaptic features are important for neuron communications in the brain. Picture in your mind, that your brain has approximately 100 billion neurons communicating with each other. This communication between neurons is referred to as a synaptic function. The dendritic spins function as a storage site for synaptic strength and assist in the transmission of electrical signals to neurons. Dendritic spins are considered to be one of the most plastic areas in the brain. Thus, the ability of the brain to change in structure and functions is partially dependent on the efficient service of the dendritic spins (van der Kolk, The neurobiolology of childhood trauma and abuse, 2003; Dookie, 2017).

Insecure Attachment and Grey Matter

The brain's neuronal cell bodies are primarily located in the grey matter. Grey matter is essential to the following functions:

muscle control, and sensory perceptions, which include hearing, seeing, memory, emotions, speech, decision making, and self-control. Consider the above features and how vital they are to our daily lives. Think of an individual who grew up in an environment that was negative and toxic, leading them to develop an insecure attachment. These individuals would have problems with sensory perceptions and muscle control due to significant reduction in grey matter (Dookie, 2017).

Insecure Attachment and Neuronal Migration

Insecure attachment leads to decreased neuronal migration, myelination, and neurogenesis. The reason neurons function and interact appropriately is directly related to neuronal migration. Neuronal migration is the process by which neurons come together to form healthy relationships. Every neuron will travel from its birthplace to a final destination. Some neurons are designed for the cerebral cortex, cerebellum, hippocampus, or spinal cord. These neurons are guided to their final destinations, slowly moving alongside a specific type of glial cell. This glial cell is called a radial glia. Radial glia is known as a cellular guide. Neuronal migration is critical for efficient brain development; so, can you imagine the damage to a child in a toxic environment. This may cause neurons not to reach their final destination; thus, there will be underdeveloped brain areas (Dookie, 2017).

Insecure Attachment and Neuronal Myelination

An insecure attachment interrupts neuronal myelination. Whenever I think of neuronal myelination, I picture a bulletproof vest that protects an individual from the impact of an incoming bullet. Myelination is the process in which fatty lipids and proteins accumulate around the neurons. Myelin is crucial to the health and function of the neurons in the brain and nervous system. One can consider myelination as the process by which the mind moves from immaturity to maturity. Take, for example, the frontal cortex. This is the last area of the adolescent brain to mature. Thus, the reason teenagers often display risky and impulsively behavior (Dookie, 2017; Fernando & Kristy, 2016; Infurna, Rivers, Reich, & Zautra, 2015).

Insecure Attachment and Neurogenesis

An insecure attachment also decreases the process of neurogenesis. Neurogenesis is the process by which new neurons are generated from neural stem cells. Neurogenesis begins in the prenatal stage and continues throughout the life-span. Children in stressful environments show slower production of neurons and a decrease in the survival of new neurons. Fewer neurons are being produced, and the neurons that are generated have a decreased survival rate. Numerous studies indicate that early life stress significantly impacts the process of neurogenesis in the hippocampus negatively.

When you think of the hippocampus, imagine the campus of a university. A university is a place to learn, consolidate, retrieve, and apply information; the hippocampus is important for memory. Given that an insecure attachment negatively impacts the process of neurogenesis, thus influencing the hippocampus and other areas of the brain, we need to pay keen attention the environment we create for children. The damage that stressful environments imposed on the brain can significantly alter the individual's life. The reality is that the process of neurogenesis is disrupted in the entire brain due to distress within the environment.

Children exposed to a toxic environment at an early stage of development will inevitably have an overactive hypothalamic-pituitary-adrenocortical axis (HPA). A toxic situation can be described as one which has inconsistent, insensitive, intrusive, inattentive, and irresponsible caregivers. Such an environment leads to attachment anxiety and avoidant attachment. Attachment anxiety is persistent worrying about being rejected and abandoned, while avoidant attachment leads to difficulties in forming close relationships, including intimate relationships. I will discuss both anxious attachment and avoidant attachment in the next section.

The activation of the hypothalamic-pituitary-adrenocortical axis (HPA), causes a reduction in cerebral volume, premature brain atrophy, brain cell density decrease, poor emotional regulation, and cortisol dysregulation. Maybe you are asking yourself, how is it that the HPA gets activated? Well, imagine a building with an alarm system.

The red rectangular box is the trigger. When the alarm is triggered, it sends a message to the 911 operator, the 911 operator calls the fire department, and the fire department sends firefighters to extinguish the flames.

Let's apply this to our brain; the trigger is the amygdala. When it is triggered by fear, it sends a message to the hypothalamus (the 911 operator). Then the hypothalamus sends a message to the pituitary gland (fire department). The pituitary gland sends a message to the adrenal gland; the adrenal gland sends firefighters (cortisol). When the fear is extinguished, the hippocampus (fire chief) sends a message to the prefrontal cortex (master control), which carries back a message to the adrenal gland to stop sending cortisol (firefighters) and the alarm is turned off. The above illustration is the ideal way in which the brain should work; however, for an individual who is exposed to a toxic environment, that is, inconsistent, insensitive, intrusive, inattentive, and irresponsible, their alarm never gets turned off, leading to hypersensitive HPA-axis.

Hypersensitive HPA axis predisposes the individual to an early onset of mental disorders, such as anxiety, depression, substance use disorder, post-traumatic stress disorder, developmental trauma disorder, and dissociation. It leads to a decrease in the GABA-A, noradrenergic, and glucocorticoid receptors, and also dysregulation in the release of corticosteroids and noradrenergic hormones in response to stress. This significantly impairs the limbic brain, especially in the early stages of development (Dookie, 2017).

Other brain areas will be highlighted that are significantly impacted by developmental trauma. The three regions are brain-derived neurotrophic factors, dopamine neurons, and the thalamus. Brain-derived neurotrophic factor (BDNF) is responsible for the survival, synaptic sprouting, neuronal migration, neuronal remodeling, differentiation, and growth of new neurons and synapses. Recent studies indicate that developmental trauma halts the functionality of BDNF. Research shows that neuroplasticity, which is activated by environmental stimuli, triggers the functionality of BDNF. It also interacts with traumatic stress to alter the brain's anatomy and thereby shifts the risk for the development of emotional psychopathology. BDNFs are the main neurotrophic proteins involved in the mediation of neuroplasticity (Dookie, 2017).

The thalamus plays an essential role in the brain's ability to restore itself. The thalamus is critical to neuroplasticity because it has global network connections in the brain. The thalamus is a sub-cortical brain structure within the forebrain, just above the midbrain. It is vital to the maintenance of consciousness and coordination. The thalamus is an essential function in the brain's ability to undergo neuroplasticity.

Developmental trauma impairs learning and memory in both children and adults. The brain neurons that are pivotal for learning and memory are the dopamine neurons. These neurons regulate learning and memory of behavioral responses that need to be stored and remembered in order to differentiate stimuli that are predictive of positive or negative outcomes. Research has hypothesized that developmental trauma can impair the ventral tegmental region (VTA) dopamine neurons. These neurons are responsible for the synthetization of dopamine. Environmental stimuli will initiate the restoration of dopamine neurons through the process of neuroplasticity (van der Kolk, The neurobiolology of childhood trauma and abuse, 2003; Van der Kolk & Pynoos, 2009).

Developmental Trauma Disorder

Developmental trauma disorder is the primary psychopathology of an insecure attachment. Developmental trauma deals with both the immediate and enduring consequences of a child's exposure to multiple shocks. These include emotional abuse, neglect, sexual abuse, physical abuse, witnessing domestic violence, ethnic cleansing, spiritual abuse, negative images of God, seeing God as being judgmental and punitive, and last but not least, war. When these traumas occur together consistently and persistently, it is called developmental trauma or cumulative trauma.

Dr. Van der Kolk, a prominent trauma specialist, used his research to propose a well-developed symptomology of developmental trauma. The symptoms of developmental trauma include disturbances in affect regulations and attachment patterns. It leads to rapid behavioral regressions and shifts in emotional states, loss of autonomous strivings, and aggressive behaviors against self and others.

A failure to achieve developmental competencies can result in loss of body regulation in the areas of sleep, eating, and self-care; altered schemas of the world, anticipatory behavior and traumatic expectations, multiple somatic problems, self-hatred and self-blame and chronic feelings of ineffectiveness (Van der Kolk & Pynoos, 2009; van der Kolk, The neurobiolology of childhood trauma and abuse, 2003).

Development trauma disorder negatively impacts the limbic-hypothalamic-pituitary-adrenal (LHPA) axis, the locus coeruleus-norepinephrine/sympathetic nervous system (SNS) or catecholamine system. These systems are fundamental to the regulation of effects. They work to encode, consolidate, and retrieve memory. When the LHPA axis is disrupted by developmental trauma, it stimulates the hypothalamus to release corticotrophin-releasing factors in the brain (CRF); this leads to a decreased branching of the hippocampal pyramidal neurons and a reduced number of hippocampal neurons (van der Kolk, The neurobiolology of childhood trauma and abuse, 2003).

Developmental trauma predisposes a survivor to a heightened risk of social problems, neuropsychiatric disorders, and physical health problems.

It significantly increases the risk of psychopathology in adulthood with complex symptomologies that effect emotional regulation, interpersonal relationships, self-perception, and psychosomatic disturbances (van der Kolk, The neurobiolology of childhood trauma and abuse, 2003).

Manifestations of Developmental Trauma in Adulthood

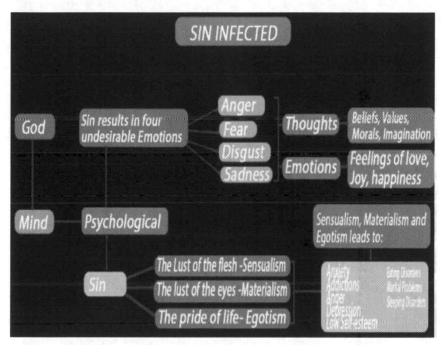

Fig 1.7

The fact is that developmental trauma disrupts the limbic-hypothalamic-pituitary-adrenal axis (LHPA axis). The result of this disruption is cognitive difficulties that permeate the entire lifespan; In other words, "from the cradle to the grave." The interruption of the cognitive functions will inevitably cause significant impairment in cognitive performance. The primary diagnosis of individuals who have experienced developmental trauma is post-traumatic stress disorder; however, the symptomology of post-traumatic stress disorder does not adequately describe the manifestation of developmental trauma.

As was mentioned above, those who experience developmental trauma are more likely to develop or to be diagnosed with a psychiatric disorder or multiple psychiatric diagnoses. These range from substance abuse disorders, depression, anxiety, personality disorders, and psychotic disorders. Individuals who have experienced emotional abuse, sexual abuse, and severe family conflicts are at a higher risk of being diagnosed with major depressive disorders. One of the main studies on childhood experience is the Adverse Childhood Experiences (ACE) study. In this study, researchers found that adults who have experienced four or more traumas are twelve times more likely to suffer from substance abuse and depression, interpersonal violence, anxiety, borderline personality disorder, chronic unemployment, and suicide.

Research has demonstrated that developmental trauma significantly contributes to interpersonal difficulties in adulthood. These include problems with trust, low interpersonal effectiveness, diminished social skills, inability to understand social interactions, poor perspective-taking abilities, an expectation of harm from others, and poor boundaries. Developmental trauma increases the risk factors for psychotic disorders.

The image above is how broken relationships affect the mental faculty. Notice the three things that emerged from a broken relationship: the lust of the flesh (sensualism), the lust of the eyes (materialism) and the pride of life (egotism). We can trace all major psychotic disorders to these three: sensualism, materialism, and egotism. Let's define these three terms. Sensualism refers to the pursuit of extreme sensual pleasure. Materialism refers to the unhealthy attachment to the persistent perusal of material possession at the expense of one's well-being and spirituality. Egotism refers to the tendency to value everything only in reference to one's personal interest.

By looking at just the definitions of these terms, you can already see how they could lead to the development of psychiatric disorders. Imagine caregivers focus more on their own pleasures, their pursuit of material possession, and self-interest. The natural result of this would be that children would be neglected and not properly attended to, thus, leading to the development of anxiety, addictions, anger, depression, low self-esteem, eating disorders, marital problems, and sleeping disorders.

This chapter highlighted the consequences of an insecure attachment on the brain. It demonstrated that an insecure attachment causes brain damage that eventfully leads to developmental trauma disorder. Developmental trauma disorder manifests itself in many forms, such as attachment anxiety, attachment avoidance, low interpersonal skills, poor boundaries, depression, anxiety, unemployment, suicidality, and cognitive impairment.

Recall from the first paragraph of the chapter that the root of insecure attachment is a broken relationship, which is the result of sin.

The section highlighted the impact of a broken relationship on the brain as a result of sin. In the next section, I will explore God's plan for restoring the human mind.

SECTION THREE: GOD'S PLAN TO RESTORE OUR MIND

The two previous sections discussed how God designed the mind and what led to the dysregulation of the mind. In this section, the focus will be primarily on God's solution to the problem of a dysregulated mind. Daniel Siegel postulated that a dysregulated mind falls into two categories, chaotic and rigid. Both chaos and rigidity are the underlying foundation to all mental disorders. Chaos and rigidity are caused due to a broken relationship with God. The moment Adam and Eve broke their relationship with God, they began to experience the chaos around them. In an effort to control the chaos, they became rigid. The chaos could be seen in their nakedness and gradual deterioration of life. Rigidity was evident in the manner in which they approached each other and God; they were determined to cover themselves with their own covering and to blame someone else for their actions.

Notice God's approach with Adam and Eve. First, He came searching for them. The reality is, there is nothing we can do that would prevent God from seeking to reconnect with us. It is through a reconnection with God that will bring healing to the mind.

CHAPTER **4**

GOD'S ATTACHMENT, AND THE BRAIN

Throughout history, God has been portrayed through different lenses in various religions. The common thread that weaves through all religion is the relationship between the worshiper and his or her deity. Christianity and Judaism are not an exception to this reality in history. In the Bible, God's people approached Him based on how they perceived that they had experienced Him in a relationship. Many thought God needed to be appeased; thus, they offered sacrifices to Him because these sacrifices would prevent God from punishing them. There were others who conceived God in a covenantal relationship in which both parties (God and humanity) are mutually responsible for various aspects of the agreed covenant. The point is that the relationship is an essential component of the connection we have with God. Thus, the way we perceive God in a relationship will determine the way we approach God and the quality of the relationship we develop with God.

At this point, I would like you to pause reading this book and spend five-to-ten minutes in reflection on your relationship with God. Here are some questions to ponder: why do I worship God, and why do I want to get to heaven?

Do we worship God because we are fearful of His judgment or do we worship God because we want to get out of this world and enter into a new one where there is peace, love, and happiness? After listening to numerous individuals over the last seventeen years giving their answers to the above questions, I have documented the following responses:

"I worship God because it is the only way to escape the judgment to come." "I worship God because I want to get out of this sin-cursed world."

"I worship God because it is the right thing to do."

"I worship God because I do not want to go to hell and burn forever."

"I worship God because He requires it."

"I worship God because I want to go to heaven."

"I worship God because I want to see my loved ones again."

"I worship God because I want to get healing from physical maladies."

"I worship because God loves me so much that I desire to be connected with Him."

"I worship God because I want to see Jesus again."

Notice the different responses; all these reactions point to the various relationships worshipers have with God. Did you know that the way we perceive God in an attachment relationship governs biopsychosocial spiritual implications of our connections to God? In other words, worshiping God should bring healing to our lives; however, the type of attachment we develop with God determines if we receive that healing or not.

The word "attachment" from the perspective of the attachment theory means the affectionate bond between an individual and an attachment figure. This is demonstrated through the child and primary attachment figure relationship. In this type of relationship, the child depends on the principal attachment figure to fulfill the following needs: safety, security, shelter, sustenance (food), love, and comfort. To conceive this from the perspective of God, attachment figures are the biological point to survival needs, the psychological aspects to the need for safety, the social points to the need for connection, and the spiritual points to the need for salvation. Here we are identifying the four basic needs of human's survival needs: safety needs, the need for connections, and the need for salvation. The attachment theory postulated that the child is attached to the primary attachment figure intrinsically, instinctively, and intuitively for the satisfaction of the needs as mentioned above. Let's explore these requirements in relation to God.

Proximity/Closeness to God

John Bowlby talked about the proximity of the child and the primary attachment figure; in his framework, this is a primal biological need. In the attachment theory, once the baby becomes mobile, the child will maintain constant eye contact with the primary attachment figure. In the Christian faith, the child is the believer. The believer can be an explorer, but for the believer to maintain a connection to God, he or she must keep eyes always on God, who is the primary attachment figure. Christianity is pivoted on the believer's desire to be connected to God. Maintaining closeness to God is the only way to grow in faith. Examine the following verses from the Bible:

"Pray without ceasing." *1 Thessalonians 5:17*

"Am I a God near at hand," says the Lord, "And not a God afar off…" *Jeremiah 23: 23*

"Draw near to God and He will draw near to you." *James 4:8*

"The Lord *is* near to all who call upon Him, to all who call upon Him in truth" *Psalm 145:18*

"But those who wait on the Lord Shall renew *their* strength; They shall mount up with wings like eagles, they shall run and not be weary, they shall walk and not faint." *Isaiah 40:31.*

Many other verses in the Bible talk about being close to God. In theology, there is a principle known as omnipresent, that is, that God is in all places at all times. Another way God's children maintain closeness to Him is through worship. Every time we assemble to worship, we get closer to

God and each other. As the believers get closer to God, their faith and trust in Him are strengthened.

Our desire to maintain proximity to God will strengthen the attachment circuitry within our brain. As children of God, we have brain networks that guarantee our bonding to God, who is our primary attachment figure. Talking to God on a daily basis will strengthen and activate the neuronal system that allows us to be intimate with God. The Bible refers to God as our father, lover, mother, and one who has a keen interest in being in a deep relationship with His people. One of the critical aspects of this relationship with God is rooted in God's compassion and loving-kindness towards us. Entering into a relationship with God allows God to instill His compassion and loving-kindness into our minds. The result of this will manifest itself in the way that we develop compassion and loving-kindness for ourselves and others.

Numerous studies have highlighted the neuronal connection between loving-kindness and compassion and its impact on the brain. There are two key areas of the brain where loving-kindness and compassion are activated: the insula and the anterior cingulate.

Recall the functions of the insula and anterior cingulate cortex from the previous chapter. Both the insula and the anterior cingulate cortex are significant communicators in our brains.

The insula detects emotion and maps its physiological symptoms within the body and makes this information available to other parts of the brain. As a communicator in the brain, the anterior cingulate cortex functions in deciding what gets attention, monitoring conflicts, making choices, and making decisions. Similar to insula, the anterior cingulate cortex will alert other brain areas to the need for increased cognitive control to resolve conflicts, make a choice, and make decisions.

The moment we accept God in our lives, we become newborn babies in Christ. As babies in Christ, we grow daily because of our constant connection to a caring and compassionate God. Growing in Christ requires that we maintain close proximity to Christ. Being close to Christ, who is loving, kind, and compassionate, helps these attributes to be imparted to us when we demonstrate loving-kindness and compassion to ourselves and those around us. This activates our insula and anterior cingulate, making us more emotionally in tune with ourselves and others. It also facilitates our abilities to manage conflicts. This suggests that loving-kindness is a crucial part of a contented life. What is clear from the preceding is that when you have a relationship with God, a secure base is created.

CHAPTER 5

INVESTIGATING GOD AND DEVOTION

God as a Secure Base

John Bowlby stated, "when an individual is confident that an attachment figure will be available to him whenever he desires it, that person will be less prone to either intense or chronic fear than will an individual who for any reason has no such confidence." Can we consider God to be a secure base? Notice some keywords in the above quotation, "confidence," "availability" and "desires." We can have the confidence that God is always available to give us the desires of our hearts according to His will for our lives.

- "Now this is the confidence that we have in Him, that if we ask anything according to His will, He hears us." 1 John 5:14
- "in whom we have boldness and access with confidence through faith in Him." Eph. 3:12
- "Let us therefore come boldly to the throne of grace, that we may obtain mercy and find grace to help in time of need." Hebrews 4:16
- "Blessed *is* the man who trusts in the Lord, And whose hope is the Lord." Jeremiah 17:7
- "being confident of this very thing, that He who has begun a good work in you will complete *it* until the day of Jesus Christ;" Philippians 1:6

Having God as a secure base allows us to approach Him with confidence, knowing the He loves us and has our best interest in mind. Through faith, we can access God's will for our lives. In confidence, we have freedom in a loving relationship with God. In confidence, he will supply all our needs. These include our relational needs, physical needs, psychological needs, and spiritual needs. As the attachment figure, children of God can rest confidently in the all-encompassing love of God.

The second word of importance in the above quotation is availability. In order for a child to develop holistically, the primary attachment figure must be available to the child. In our relationship with God, it is no different. To form a secure attachment to God, He must make Himself available to us, His Children.

- "For I am persuaded that neither death nor life, nor angels nor principalities nor powers, nor things present nor things to come, nor height nor depth, nor any other created thing, shall be able to separate us from the love of God which is in Christ Jesus our Lord." Romans 8:38-39
- "Therefore, I say to you, do not worry about your life, what you will eat or what you will drink; nor about your body, what you will put on. Is not life more than food and the body more than clothing? Look at the birds of the air, for they neither sow nor reap nor gather into barns; yet your heavenly Father feeds them. Are you not of more value than they? Which of you by worrying can add one cubit to his stature? "So why do you worry about clothing? Consider the lilies of the field, how they grow: they neither toil nor spin; and yet I say to you that even Solomon in all his glory was not arrayed like one of these. Now if God so clothes the grass of the field, which today is, and tomorrow is thrown into the oven, *will He* not much more *clothe* you, O you of little faith? "Therefore, do not worry, saying, 'What shall we eat?' or 'What shall we drink?' or 'What shall we wear?' For after all these things the Gentiles seek. For your heavenly Father knows that you need all these things. But seek first the kingdom of God and His righteousness, and all these things shall be added to you. Therefore, do not worry about tomorrow, for tomorrow

will worry about its own things. Sufficient for the day *is* its own trouble." Matthew 6:25-34

- "Do you not know that you are the temple of God and *that* the Spirit of God dwells in you?" 1 Corinthians 3:16
- "The Lord your God in your midst, The Mighty One, will save; He will rejoice over you with gladness, He will quiet *you* with His love, He will rejoice over you with singing." Zephaniah 3:17
- "Behold, I stand at the door and knock. If anyone hears My voice and opens the door, I will come into him and dine with him, and he with Me. " Revelation 3:20
- Where can I go from Your Spirit? Or where can I flee from Your presence? If I ascend into heaven, you *are* there; If I make my bed in hell, behold, you *are there. If* I take the wings of the morning, *And* dwell in the uttermost parts of the sea, Even there Your hand shall lead me, And Your right hand shall hold me. Psalm 139:7-10
- "that Christ may dwell in your hearts through faith; that you, being rooted and grounded in love," Ephesians 3:17
- "*Am* I a God near at hand," says the Lord, "And not a God afar off? Can anyone hide himself in secret places, So I shall not see him?" says the Lord; "Do I not fill heaven and earth?" says the Lord. Jeremiah 23:23-24
- "Jesus answered and said to him, "If anyone loves Me, he will keep My word; and My Father will love him, and We will come to him and make Our home with him." John 14:23

These are just a few verses in the Bible that illustrate that God is always available to us. In the book of Isaiah chapter 65:24, the writer declares, "before they call I will answer; while they are still speaking, I will hear." God promised His children that He would never leave them nor forsake them, but He will be with us to the end of the earth. The reality is that nothing can pull God away from us.

The third word I highlighted in the above quotation is "desires". The attachment figure must understand and aid in the desires of their children. The primary attachment figure must be in tune with the child to know the hopes of the child. Children desire to be loved, cared for, nurtured, happy, contented, safe, etc. The Bible stated that, if we delight in the Lord, He will give us the desires of our hearts (Psalm 37:4). God knows that your heart desires to be safe, to be happy, to be loved, to be cared for, and to have peace in difficult times. Thus, as our caregiver, he will see and supply us our desires.

God said, I love you with an everlasting love, my plan makes you happy and prosperous, cast your care on me because I care for you.

Having God as a secure base gives us the confidence that He is available to us to attend to the desires of our hearts. Therefore, we do not need to be fearful.

- "Fear not, for I *am* with you; Be not dismayed, for I *am* your God. I will strengthen you, Yes, I will help you, I will uphold you with My righteous right hand." Isaiah 41:10
- "Be strong and of good courage, do not fear nor be afraid of them; for the Lord your God, He *is* the One who goes with you. He will not leave you nor forsake you." Deuteronomy 31:6
- "Peace I leave with you, my peace I give to you; not as the world gives do, I give to you. Let not your heart be troubled, neither let it be afraid." John 14:27
- "For God has not given us a spirit of fear, but of power and of love and of a sound mind." 2 Timothy 1:7
- "There is no fear in love; but perfect love casts out fear, because fear involves torment. But he who fears has not been made perfect in love." 1 John 4:18
- "But now, thus says the Lord, who created you, O Jacob, And He who formed you, O Israel: "Fear not, for I have redeemed you; I have called *you* by your name; You *are* Mine." Isaiah 43:1
- "Have I not commanded you? Be strong and of good courage; do not be afraid, nor be dismayed, for the Lord your God *is* with you wherever you go." Joshua 1:9

God as a Haven of Safety

When we have confidence in God, that He is available to us to supply the desires of our hearts according to His riches in glory, we will have nothing to fear because God is our refuge and strength, a present help in the time of challenge. God is our rock and our strength. This leads to

Bowlby's principle that the attachment figure serves as a haven of safety in times of danger or threat. According to Bowlby, threat comes in three forms: frightening or alarming environment; illness, injury, or fatigue; and separation or risk of separation from an attachment figure.

We can trust God to be a place of safety for us; this does not mean that difficult things will not happen. What it means is that when the frightening and alarming environmental threats occur, God will give us the strength to manage. When cancer or other life-threatening diseases hit our loved ones or us, or when a loved one dies or is having to leave us for some other reason, God promised that he would never leave us nor forsake us. In the book of Isaiah, the prophet declares, "when you pass through the rough waters, I will be with you, and the roaring rivers, they shall not overflow you:

When you walk through the fire, you shall not be burned; neither flame touch you" (Isaiah 43:2). The important thing to note is that the text did not say that we will be taken out of the waters, fire or river, but when we go through them, God will be a safe-haven for us.

CHAPTER

NEUROPLASTICITY: THE BRAIN'S ABILITY TO CHANGE

In chapter three I discussed the implications of an insecure attachment on the brain. Can you imagine that in years gone by it was believed that those brain damages that resulted from developmental trauma could never be restored? I am so happy that God is a God of change. Neuroscience has recently discovered that our brain has the ability to change and the power to change our brain rests in our hands. This change process is known as neuroplasticity.

However, before I discuss neuroplasticity, I want to bring your attention to how to initiate the process of neuroplasticity. The starting point is mind transformation. To transform the mind, we must explore what the mind is and what are the faculties of the mind. God desires to change our mind and restore humans to His divine image. Neuroplasticity is God's way of restoring the mind through the healing of the four faculties of the mind.

Neuroplasticity

The term "plasticity" was first introduced by William James as it relates to the nervous system. It was later postulated by Eugenio Tanzi that plasticity could take place between neurons. Ernesto Lugaro described the linkage between neuronal plasticity and synaptic plasticity. It was later hypothesized that plasticity is the result of connections between cortical neurons. Neuroplasticity is the brain's ability to change and adapt to environmental stimuli. Research has demonstrated that an enriched environment can change the structural and chemical composition of the brain. The fact is, the brain has the ability to change throughout the lifespan, that is, it has the aptitude to restructure and reorganize in response to physical and cognitive activity.

Neuroplasticity allows the brain to restore functions in areas that have been compromised due to developmental trauma. The brain can respond and adapt to environmental challenges and encompasses a series of functional and structural mechanisms that may lead to neuronal remodeling, formation of new synapses, and birth of new neurons. Neuroplasticity works via a process known as neurogenesis. Neurogenesis refers to the development of newly born neurons that are generated from progenitors to integrate into the neuronal network functionally (Dookie, 2017; Grossman, Zucker, Spinazzola, & Hopper, 2017).

Neuroplasticity is God's fail-safe to restoring the human mind. As was discussed in the previous chapter, the mind consists of four faculties: the physical (emphasis on the brain), the psychological, spiritual, and relational. Neuroplasticity works through each department to bring healing to the mind. Developmental trauma impacts each of the above faculties. Often, individuals who have been traumatized have a negative view of God. Their question is, why did God not intervene in my situation and prevent the pain that I experience? They will say, why should I worship when Him was never there for me? In these cases, trauma has significantly damaged the spiritual faculty.

Trauma negatively impacts the relational faculty of individuals who have experienced an insecure attachment. They can develop both anxious attachment and avoidant attachment. Research has demonstrated that attachment anxiety is associated with increased reactivity to both attachment related and nonattachment related stressors in adults. In light of the reality that developmental trauma severely damages the four faculties of the mind, God's plan is to restore the mind through the process of neuroplasticity.

Anxious attachment activates brain areas that are involved in the generation of adverse effect and memories and a down-regulation of the brain areas that are responsible for aiding negative emotions.

Anxious attachment leads individuals to be self-critical, insecure, and self-doubting. Getting reassurance and approval from others is paramount to their psychological well-being.

In interpersonal relationships, they are preoccupied with the thought that they will be rejected, thus, making them worry and have difficulties trusting others. They are clingy and overly dependent on their partners. Individuals with anxious attachment develop elaborate plans on how to avoid rejections, but because of their clinginess, they often perceived themselves to be rejected even if that is not the case.

Adults with anxious attachment tend to doubt their capacity for attending the needs of others due to their own extreme anxiety about their ability to meet the other person's needs. Take, for example, a mother who has a history of anxious attachment; she will see her child crying for food and know that the child is in need of food but because of her own anxiety, she doubts her ability to attend to the child's need. The child then absorbs the internal world of the mother, and he/she starts to develop an anxious attachment. The child is responding to the mirror neurons of the mother; in other words, the child is mirroring the caregiver. This leads the child to become confused about his or her own sense of self.

The second way in which an insecure attachment impacts the relational faculty is in the formation of avoidant attachment. Avoidant attachment is the tendency to downplay or suppress one's emotions as a way to defend oneself from dealing with intimacy and feelings that are threatening. These individuals use suppression as a defense mechanism.

Someone who has an avoidant attachment style will avoid closeness. Their independence and self-sufficiency are more important than intimacy. Think of someone who finds it extremely difficult and uncomfortable sharing feelings with intimate partners or those with whom they have close relationships. In a similar fashion, an insecure attachment damages the physiological faculty; this includes both the cortical and subcortical. These brain areas were examined in chapter two.

Insecure attachment causes disintegration in the brain, that is, the brain area does not communicate in the way it was designed to function. Think of your prefrontal cortex not communicating effectively with the limbic system. This means that our emotions are not governed by the rational or executive part of the brain. Individuals who have experienced trauma would have an overactive HPA-axis. This implies that the parasympathetic nervous system would be in overdrive. This would limit the cerebral blood flow to the prefrontal cortex, thus, decoupling the connection between the executive and the emotional brain (Davidson & Lutz, 2008; Davidson R., 2008; Dookie, 2017).

It is difficult to have a healthy spiritual experience if your view of God is influenced by an insecure attachment. I remember one young lady who could not perceive God as a father because of her past relationship with her biological father. In my work with her, I helped her to understand what the ideal father should be like and what God is like being our father.

Having this understanding enabled her to begin the journey of seeing God as a father who is loving, kind, caring, and nurturing.

Another way that an insecure attachment impairs spiritual connection to God is our view of God. Individuals who see God as being judgmental and punitive will see God as a person to fear. Worship that is fear-based will damage the mind rather than heal it. This means that we might have to change the way we think about and worship God. Neuroplasticity engages the brain in restoring these faculties of the mind. A healthy relationship with God and others will bring change to the structure and function of the brain. Envision this: if you start to change your thinking patterns, you can improve the structural and functional capabilities of your brain. The process of neuroplasticity is deeply intertwined with the transformation of the mind. God's original plan for our lives is to transform our minds. The following are some bible verses that emphasize God's plan to transform our minds:

- And do not be conformed to this world, but be transformed by the renewing of your mind, that you may prove what *is* that good and acceptable and perfect will of God (Romans 12:2)
- Create in me a clean heart, O God, and renew a steadfast spirit within me. (Psalm 51:10)

- Let this mind be in you which was also in Christ Jesus, who, being in the form of God, did not consider it. (Phil 2:5)
- For God has not given us a spirit of fear, but of power and of love and of a sound mind. (2 Timothy 1:7)
- Therefore, gird up the loins of your mind, be sober, and rest *your* hope fully upon the grace that is to be brought to you at the revelation of Jesus Christ; (1 Peter 1:13)
- …But we have the mind of Christ. (1 Corinthians 2:16)

The key theme in these verses is that God desires to transform our minds and give us the mind of Christ. Christ has a healthy relationship with both His Father and humanity. This is the relationship that God desires for His children.

CHAPTER 7

ESTABLISHING BIBLICAL MEDITATION

The Bible highlighted various principles that God has given to us to restore our relationship with Him. By repairing our relationship with God, we begin the process of rebuilding our minds; this leads to healing the brain from the impact of developmental trauma, anxiety, addictions, and depression. There are seven biblical principles that I will explore that can be used to restore the brain from the impact of development trauma, such as addiction, anxiety, and depression. Biblical meditation includes visualization, focused attention, opening, praying, deep breathing, loving-kindness, and compassion. I will explore each component of biblical reflection regarding the healing of the brain from psychological distress that resulted from developmental trauma.

Biblical Definition of Meditation

Before proceeding to the principles of biblical meditation, I want to establish taxonomy and the definition of biblical meditation. You may ask, why establish a taxonomy and description of biblical meditation? A taxonomic nomenclature of meditation will establish the scientific reliability of meditation. On the other hand, a definition of biblical meditation will distinguish it from other forms of meditation.

The term meditation has been used in numerous cultures around the globe. In recent years, it has been made very popular by the eastern culture because they have been using it to bring healing to the brain and the body. I will first begin with a taxonomic nomenclature of meditation.

Taxonomic Nomenclature of Meditation

In developing a taxonomic classification of meditation, there must be some parameters utilized to formulate this theoretical paradigm. Research done by Nash and Newberg postulated that a scientifically sound taxonomy of meditation ought to be pivoted on a third-person approach. This section is primarily a review of the work of Nash and Newberg in establishing meditation as a scientific entity. The purpose of developing a taxonomy of meditation is essential for reliability and validity. Anything that presents itself to be scientific must be established to be reliable and valid.

In the work of Aristotle and Linnaeus, they developed a theoretical paradigm known as "essentialist." This framework to scientific taxonomy postulated that every entity has an essential feature that makes up the type of entity. Essentialism argued that the features of the entity are its real essence. "The real essence of an entity occurs in all and only entities of that type, and it helps us understand why entities of that type do the sorts of things they do."

Thus, the first step towards a taxonomy of meditation is to determine the real and functional essence of meditation, given that it is meditation that we desire to taxonomize (Newberg, et al., 2010; Newberg & Waldman, How God changes your brain, 2010).

According to Nash and Newberg, the functional essence of meditation is hinged on the most salient goal, that is, enhanced mental state (EMS). Considering the above framework, the first task is to establish the functional essence of meditation. To determine the operational principle of meditation, this must be derived from the primary goals and purposes of meditation. This requires the specific techniques that are used to accomplish the most salient goals. Bearing in mind the plethora of research around meditation, it can be concluded that the basic essence of meditation is to attain to an enhanced mental state (EMS). An enhanced psychological state would activate all parts of the brain. In doing so, it would increase cerebral blood flow throughout the brain (Newberg & Waldman, How God changes your brain, 2010).

Numerous external and internal factors need to be taken into consideration to obtain an enhanced mental state. This includes experience and expertise, motivation, current state of mind and body, intoxicants, intentions, and mental condition. Recall the phrase from the definition of the essentialist approach "…it helps us understand why entities of that type do the sorts of things they do."

This indicates that the entity (meditation) helps us to understand why entities (meditation) of that type do the sorts of things they do. In regard to meditation, this is demonstrated in the laboratory environment, where scientists can measure the intended outcomes by analyzing brain activities during meditation. This is reminiscent of the concept that a given method can possess a specific intended or targeted outcome (Newberg & Waldman, How God changes your brain, 2010; Dookie, 2017).

In developing taxonomy, it is necessary to establish terminology. Thus, there needs to be a taxonomy nomenclature for the meditation method. In their work, Nash and Newberg proposed a classification of meditation method that constitutes three domains: the affective domain, the null domain, and the cognitive domain. In the affective domain method, the techniques of loving-kindness and compassion are used to enhance the emotional state. Loving-kindness and compassion are key features of Christian meditation and prayer. The null domain method utilizes dissociation techniques. This technique is used to attain the enhanced empty state (EES). The third domain is the cognitive domain. This method is cognitively directed and is used to increase the cognitive state. The domains are based on the essentialism taxonomy framework, in collaboration with a third-person approach. These domains are viewed through the prism of affective and cognitive paradigm (Newberg & Waldman, How God changes your brain, 2010).

In establishing classification methods for meditation, it is also critical to devise a taxonomy nomenclature for resultant states. Nash and Newberg identified three resultant states: enhanced cognitive states, enhanced affective states, and enhanced non-cognitive/non-affective states. The enhanced cognitive state has to do with the practitioner's ability to focus on a single object. The enhanced affective state is directly related to the practitioner's phenomenological experience with feelings, such as loving-kindness or compassion. The enhanced non-cognitive/non-affective state is akin to emptiness, that is, no phenomenological content (Newberg & Waldman, How God changes your brain, 2010).

To further elucidate these three domains of the taxonomy nomenclature of meditation method, some sub-divisions are necessary. These sub-divisions can be considered the techniques by which the meditation method is employed. These sub-divisions include cognitive strategies, the objects of attention, belief system, visual position, auditory position, body position, focusing on whether the practitioners are static or kinetic, whether the practice is intrinsic or extrinsic, and if there are specific breathing requirements.

This section explored the advancement of a taxonomy for meditation. The taxonomy takes a third-person approach because this is more reliable and scientific. The classification of the meditative method has three sections:

the functional essence of meditation methods, a terminology of reflective practices, and the resultant states. Therefore, using the above framework, we can conclude that meditation is both a spiritual endeavor and has scientific results. In the next section, I will discuss meditation in general and then proceed to develop a biblical definition of meditation.

Meditation in General

The evolution of meditative science is making extraordinary contributions to the field of clinical psychotherapeutic practice. Meditation is becoming a growing phenomenon in the major urban centers of the world. The term meditation has become a generic term, referring to secular, spiritual, and/or religious contemplative activities. Scholars in the field of meditative practice are still grappling with establishing a universally agreeable definition for the field. A search of contemplative practice in *PubMed Central* produced 813 references to contemplative practices. Of these 813 references to contemplative practice, only four articles made direct references to an operational definition of a contemplative practice. This is an indication that contemplative practices are not clearly defined.

Hence, this section will investigate themes that emerge and relate to defining or describing contemplative practice.

Different philosophical constructs emerge from a modern conceptualization of meditation, such as awareness, attention, relaxation, self-transcendence, and mindfulness.

The preliminary conceptualization of meditation was seen through the lens of relaxation. In this framework, the practitioner seeks to devoid the mind of thought activity to develop consciousness without considering mental silence. The proposal that relaxation is an integral component towards a functional definition of meditation cannot be denied, but total elimination of thought is contraindicated to the principle of mental silence.

Research indicated that attention is an essential constituent of what constitutes functional meditation. There are two fundamental categories of attention. They are focused attention (FA) and open monitoring. According to Dan Siegel, attention is the process that regulates the flow of information and can either be with awareness or without awareness (Davidson R. J., 2016).

Another primary component of meditation is mindfulness. In mindfulness, the practitioner's goal is to develop an awareness of the present moment's experience of perceptible mental process. The practice of mindfulness seeks to engage the mind to pay attention and focus on becoming aware of the present with intention and purpose. The key terms that are emerging from the exploration thus far are concentration, relaxation, consciousness, mindfulness, intention, purpose, mind, attention, and awareness. This is indicative of a fundamental challenge that contemplative scientists struggle with, that is, the terminological dilemma.

With all these terms, it becomes very challenging to establish a comprehensive definition of meditation (Davidson R. J., 2016).

The common denominator of most definitions of meditation is rooted in self-regulation, that is, the capability to orient, shift, and maintain

Dr. Courtney Dookie

attention in collaboration with metacognitive awareness. Modes of existential awareness is another aspect of meditation. It encompasses the cumulative changes in attention, effective and conceptual elements of metacognitive self-regulatory process, which are modulated by motivational and contextual factors of meditation practice.

Meditation is also multidisciplinary; It considers cultural, sociological, neurobiological, psychological and spiritual aspects. An aspect of existential awareness that is pertinent to meditation is attention. Attention can be described as observing thoughts, feelings, and somatosensory experiences. Perception, attention, purpose, staying in the present moment, and non-judgmental observation are fundamental elements that are constitutional to meditation. Contemplative scientists postulated that meditation is the discipline of attention. Another area to consider in establishing a workable definition of meditation is attitude. The components of attitude are quality of emotional openness, curiosity, and non-judgmental stances (Davidson R. J., 2016).

Some scholars defined meditation as having stages. Some researchers proposed three stages of meditation: early, middle, and advanced. Others proposed six stages: normal, intention to begin, preliminaries, method enhanced mental state, and intention to finish. In using these steps, they postulated that meditation is a dynamic process and believed that participation in this process is what defined meditation.

Neuroscientist Richard Davidson indicated that meditation is a complex emotional and regulatory strategy developed for various ends, including the cultivation of well-being and emotional balance. Davidson identified three components of meditation: Focus Attention, Mindfulness, and Open Monitoring. In establishing a practical definition for meditation, it must have at its core the goal of cultivating well-being for the practitioners. According to Davidson, well-being that is facilitated through meditative practices has four basic keys: resilience, outlook, attention, and generosity (Davidson & Lutz, 2008).

In this section, I highlighted various components that are essential for a working definition of meditation. Some of the key elements underscored are awareness, attention, relaxation, self-transcendent, mindfulness, focus attention and opening, self-regulatory, modes of existential awareness, and motivational/intentional and contextual factors, purposeful, present moment, non-judgmental observation, and the stages approach.

Now that the essential components of what constitutes meditation have been explored and established, a discussion of biblical meditation will follow.

CHAPTER 8

BIBLICAL MEDITATION

The formality of Christian meditation was developed in the West by the early monastic orders sometime during the twelfth century by Guigo II. He was a Carthusian monk. Guigo II proposed four levels of practice. Level one, "lectio," was slowly reading the biblical text. Level two, "meditation," was pondering the deeper meaning of the text. Level three, "oratio," was spontaneous prayer. Level four, "contemplatio," was wordlessly focusing on God's love (Newberg & Waldman, How God changes your brain, 2010).

According to the Holman Illustrated Bible Dictionary, meditation is defined as "the act of calling to mind some supposition, pondering upon it, and correlating it to one's own life. The primary biblical reference to meditation is found in the Hebrew Scriptures, especially in the psalms. There are two root words in the Hebrew Scriptures for meditation: "hagah" and "siach." The word "hagah" refers to a gentle cooing. From this root word, it has been postulated that Hebrew meditation consists of frequently reciting scriptures with a low sounding voice. In the Brown-Drive-Briggs, "hagah" is defined as to murmur in pleasure or anger, to ponder, imagine, talk, mutter, and study.

The second root word, "siach", means "to be occupied with" or "concerned about." This element of meditation denotes the reading of scriptures and holding its principle in mind until it becomes the chief principle of life, that is taking scriptures of love, joy, peace, hope, victories through challenges; triumph over tragedy and lack of faith; and allowing the mind to be occupied with these principles until they become a part of the person. This same principle of meditation is seen in the New Testament scriptures. Brown, Driver, and Briggs defined "siach" as reflection, devotion, beliefs, meditation, musing, study, and prayer (Brown, Driver, & Briggs, 2008).

Biblical meditation seeks to engage the mind. Thus, when a practitioner engages in biblical meditation and activates the mind, the mind, in turn, allows the flow of positive thoughts, actions, and words. In Psalm chapter one of the Old Testament scripture, the author described a meditative practice that engages the mind, heart and the purpose of life. It is a thoughtful practice that calls for the devotion of mind, heart, and life. Biblical meditation is centered on the sacred text, which is the Bible, and includes both the Old Testament and the New Testament.

Biblical meditation is focused on God Himself, that is, on a deep longing for God. The practitioner who engages in biblical meditation believes that God will meet their biopsychosocial-spiritual needs.

A crucial element of biblical meditation is that the practitioner prepares for the session by reading the sacred text (Bible), to allow the mind to ponder and grasp the principles that are inherent within the text/passage (Brown, Driver, & Briggs, 2008).

As is common in all three monotheistic religions, meditation is the act of reflecting on God's past actions in provision, protection, comfort, assurance, and love. Another aspect of biblical meditation that emerges from the Hebrew word "hagah" is the making of sound. In the Christian tradition, this is done through singing and the verbal repetition of the word of God. In light of what is being discussed so far, biblical meditation can be defined as a thoughtful focusing of attention on God's word through scripture, His character of love, morality, and compassion, using silence or vocalization, to produce positive impacts on the practitioner's thoughts, feelings, and actions (Brown, Driver, & Briggs, 2008; Dookie, 2017).

There are many ways to compare biblical meditation to other forms of meditation. The reality is that the vast majority of neuro-biopsychological research on meditation is centered on the eastern practice of meditation. The first commonality of biblical meditation to other meditative exercises is that they all engage in the process of seeking presence. Secondly, they all employ a method of dwelling on something or someone. In biblical meditation, this would be "God" or "the Bible." Hence, the dwelling is the common factor.

Thirdly, the seeking, the pursuit of a different state, and the effect of attention or inattention are all characteristics of meditative practice in general. There are other aspects too, and for this, we have to go back to the root words for biblical meditation. Words such as, to murmur in pleasure or anger, to ponder, imagine, talk, mutter, study, reflect, devotion, beliefs, meditation, contemplation, attention, musing, study, and prayer (Dookie, 2017).

There are various key components of biblical meditation; however, the most primal component of biblical meditation is union with Christ. Union with Christ gives the biblical meditation practitioner the sense of the real presence of Christ, in a moment by moment experience with the divine. The biblical meditator believes that upon baptism they become one spirit, being united in Christ (1 Cor. 12:13; 1 Cor. 6:17). A central tenet of biblical meditation is that the practitioner must believe in the principles of the Bible.

Biblical meditation has three modes of presence: definitive, repletive, and circumscriptive. The definitive style points at being present in the moment at a specific location, while the repletive way points at being present on earth in a global sense and in heaven in a spiritual sense. Circumscriptive mode is real visible presence, that is, the interpersonal relationship members of a church or family members.

In light of the recent explosion in contemplative science, there has been limited research that focuses on contemplative practices within Christianity. For instance, in the masterpiece on the taxonomy of meditation by Nash and Newberg, they applied their principles to nine meditative methods, none of which are related to Christianity. I hypothesize that the above definition and taxonomy of meditation can be applied to Christian meditation.

The thematic, scriptural, and devotional approach to meditation in Christianity unitized a substantial number of technical elements. It is important to clarify what is meant by technical factors; technical details can fall into five general categories. It is a deliberate practice with the end goal of creating specific effects; it has clearly defined procedures with partial lucidity; it is deliberately structured within time (particular time is set aside for the practice); it is continuous; and its effects are psychobiological.

There are twenty original verses in the bible that use the word meditation; the verses are as follows:

1. Genesis 24:63 And Isaac went out to meditate in the field toward evening. And he lifted up his eyes and saw and behold; there were camels coming.
2. Joshua 1:8 This Book of the Law shall not depart from your mouth, but you shall meditate on it day and night, so that you may be careful to do according to all that is written in it.

For then you will make your way prosperous, and then you will have good success.

3. Psalm 1:2 but his delight is in the law of the Lord, and on his law, he meditates day and night.
4. Psalm 5:1 Give ear to my words, O Lord, Consider my meditation.
5. Psalm 19:14 [14] Let the words of my mouth, and the meditation of my heart be acceptable in your sight, O Lord, my rock and my redeemer.
6. Psalm 49:3 My mouth shall speak wisdom; the meditation of my heart shall be understanding.
7. Psalm 63:6 when I remember you upon my bed and meditate on you in the watches of the night;
8. Psalm 77:12 I will ponder all your work and meditate on your mighty deeds.
9. Psalm 104:34 May my meditation be pleasing to him, for I rejoice in the Lord.
10. Psalm 119:15 I will meditate on your precepts and fix my eyes on your ways.
11. Psalm 119:23 Even though princes sit plotting against me, your servant will meditate on your statutes.

12. Psalm 119:48 I will lift up my hands toward your commandments, which I love, and I will meditate on your statutes.
13. Psalm 119:78 Let the insolent be put to shame because they have wronged me with falsehood; as for me, I will meditate on your precepts.
14. Psalm 119:97 Oh how I love your law! It is my meditation all day.
15. Psalm 119:99 I have more understanding than all my teachers, for your testimonies are my meditation.
16. Psalm 119:148 My eyes are awoken before the watches of the night, that I may meditate on your promise.
17. Psalm 143:5 I remember the days of old; I meditate on all that you have done; I ponder the work of your hands.
18. Isaiah 33:18 Your heart will meditate on terror: "Where *is* the scribe? Where *is* he who weighs? Where *is* he who counts the towers?"
19. Luke 21:14 Settle it therefore in your minds not to meditate beforehand how to answer,
20. 1 Timothy 4:15 Meditate on these things; give yourself entirely to them, that your progress may be evident to all.

The key themes of meditation in these verses are the law of Love, the word of Love, the works of Love, and the way of Love. Jesus, in responding to the religious leaders of the time about the divine constitution of the law said, "You shall love the Lord your God with all your heart, with all your soul, and with all your mind. This is *the* first and greatest commandment. And *the* second *is* like it: 'You shall love your neighbor as yourself.' (Matthew 22:34-39). The central focus of the Law is love; the Bible tells us the God is Love.

Thus, biblical meditation is centered on God's love towards us and our love towards self and others. This kind of meditation includes loving-kindness, compassion, visualization of love, focusing attention on God/ awareness, openly monitoring our hearts, praying for self, others and the universe, breathing in the love, peace, joy, faithfulness of God/relaxation. These are the elements of biblical meditation that will be explored regarding neuroplasticity and the healing of psychological pains in later chapters.

9

HEALING THE BRAIN AND THE MIND THROUGH BIBLICAL MEDITATION

In this chapter, I will present evidence that biblical meditation can be used to heal the four faculties of the mind. Particular attention will be given to the physical department (brain). The outline of this chapter will be as follows: a summary of the impact of non-biblical meditation on the brain and the role that belief in God plays in practicing biblical meditation. I will go over how to use biblical meditation to heal the mind while implementing the following principles: visualization, focus attention, opening monitoring, praying, deep breathing, loving-kindness, and biblical compassion.

Impact of Non-Biblical Meditation on the Brain

Over the last three decades, numerous studies have explored the effects of meditation on the brain. Meditation activates the medial prefrontal cortex (MPFC), anterior cingulate cortex (ACC), and the posterior cingulate cortex (PCC). These are areas of the brain that are deactivated by trauma. Meditation increases the functional connectivity of the frontal cortices.

Meditation activates the parasympathetic nervous system, thus, lowering heart rates, blood pressure, respiratory rate, and oxygen metabolism. Meditative practices increase activity in the orbitofrontal cortex.

There is a growing body of research supporting the hypothesis that meditation changes the structure and function of the brain. Cognitive neuroscience is linked to a greater thickness of the anterior parts of the corpus callosum. Meditation increases both the grey and white matter and studies have established that meditation reduces amygdala responses to emotional stimuli. Traumatized survivors often would respond negatively to an emotional sensation that reminds them of the trauma; however, contemplative practice down-regulates the amygdala, thus reducing the emotional responsiveness.

The Role Belief in God Plays in Practicing Biblical Meditation

Numerous studies have explored the implication of beliefs and non-beliefs in meditative practice. The research indicates that those who accept some specific religious belief to be true, for example, "God is love" will have greater blood-oxygen level-dependent signals in the ventromedial prefrontal cortex (VMPFC), anterior insula (AI), left insula, ventral striatum, hippocampus, Para hippocampal gyrus, temporal pole, dorsal lateral prefrontal cortex (DLPFC) and retrosplenial cortex.

The opposite is true; for those who do not believe that "God is love", even if they meditate on the concept, it will not activate the above brain areas. These brain areas are responsible for learning, cognitive and executive functions, and also emotional regulation associated with psychological distress (Dookie, 2017).

Research suggests that those who believe in the essence of their meditative practice get more benefits from the exercise. Christian beliefs and practices increase activity in the dorsolateral prefrontal cortex. Trust in the fundamental principles of love, mercy, compassion, kindness, forgiveness, cheerfulness, and faithfulness as taught in the Bible increase activities in the anterior cingulate cortex (ACC) and increase white matter. The hippocampus, which is crucial for memory encoding and retrieval, is an area of the brain that is negatively impacted by complex trauma. Research indicates that to believe and contemplate on the above biblical principles will facilitate neuroplasticity in the hippocampus. The hippocampus structure is more substantial in individuals who believe in the healthy biblical tenets of their religious community than those who do not believe (Dookie, 2017).

Research informs us that healthy religious beliefs about the self and God increases blood flow to the ventromedial prefrontal cortex (VMPFC) and dorsolateral prefrontal cortex (DLPFC); however, individuals who consider themselves to be non-religious have decreased blood flow to the VMPFC and DLPFC.

Religious beliefs in comparison to the lack of it show higher activity in the hippocampus, Para hippocampal gyrus, middle temporal gyrus, temporal pole, and retrosplenial cortex. The evidence lucidly implied that those who believe in a loving, compassionate, caring, and faithful God are at an advantage over those who do not believe in God. This is particularly evident in the healing from complex trauma, anxiety, depression, and substance abuse via the process of neuroplasticity (Dookie, 2017).

Faith in God will function to activate the parasympathetic nervous system. The parasympathetic nervous system is one of the two divisions of the autonomic nervous system; it operates to bring the body to rest. The sympathetic nervous system, which is the other part of the autonomic nervous system, is responsible for the fight or flight response in the body. The fight or flight response is activated by distress, anxiety, fear, and trauma. When these psychological stressors enable the sympathetic nervous system, it is the parasympathetic that works to restore the body from the extreme tension to rest. A healthy belief system can function to stimulate the actions of the parasympathetic nervous system. This, in turn, shuts off the amygdala and brings the body back to rest.

It must be noted that to receive the neurological benefits of believing in God, those beliefs must be healthy. Believing that God is judgmental, punitive, and out to get you for the wrongs you have done, will not produce the above benefits.

A robust belief system is one in which God is seen as a supreme lover of humanity and has our best interest in His mind.

CHAPTER 10

MEDITATION AND THE HEALING OF THE PHYSICAL FACULTY

Meditating on God's word through scripture, His character of love, morality, and compassion, using silence or vocalization, will produce positive impacts in our lives; it will strengthen thought patterns, feelings, and ultimately the way we behave. Meditation within the biblical context uses the same method of practice but the object of meditation is different. Methods refer to mindfulness, focus attention (FA), open monitoring (OM), loving-kindness, and compassion. The focus of biblical meditation is on Jesus Christ and the principles that are taught by Him in the Bible.

Neuroimaging Data Showing CBF to Frontal Lobe and Thalamic

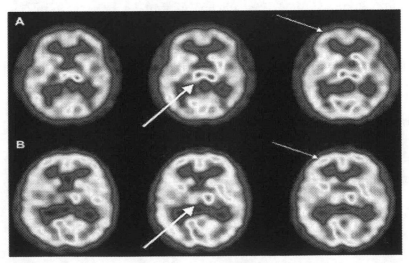

Figure 1.8 region

Fig. 1. Cerebral Blood Flow (CBF) is represented as red > yellow > green > blue) from a non-meditator (A) and a long-term meditator (B). These images demonstrate increased CBF in the frontal lobes bilaterally (thin arrows) in the long-term meditator compared to the non-meditator. Also, there is a marked asymmetry in the thalamic activity (thick arrows) in the long-term meditator rather than relatively symmetric thalamic activity in the non-meditator. Adapted from "Cerebral blood flow differences between long-term meditators and non-meditators," by Andrew B. Newberg, Nancy Wintering, Mark R. Waldman, Daniel Amen, Dharma S. Khalsa and Abass Alavi, 2010, Consciousness and Cognition, p. 4. Copyright 2010 by Elsevier Inc.

Meditation Activates the Frontal Lobe

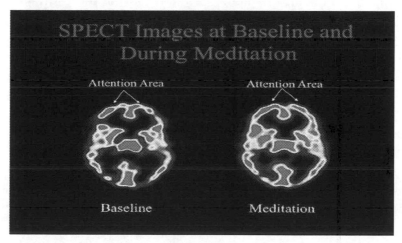

Fig. 1.9

Single photon emission computed tomography (SPECT), blood flow. The more blood flows a brain area has, the more active it is (red > yellow > green > blue > black). The image illustrated that the frontal lobe which is implicated in focus attention and concentration is more active during meditation (increase red activity). Adapted from, http://www.Andrewnewberg.com/research, by Andrew B. Newberg, 2017.

In the above image, you will notice that there is an increase in cerebral blood flow to the prefrontal cortex in individuals who practice meditation consistently. Remember that the prefrontal cortex is responsible for making plans, setting goals, formulating intentions, and emotional regulation. If meditation increases cerebral blood flow to the prefrontal cortex, it suggested that it is essential to have a meditative practice on a daily routine. Think of the fact that you will be able to make better decisions in your life decisions about your family, community, and society overall.

Neuroimaging studies support the postulation that meditation increases activity in the frontal lobe and thalamic regions. There is evidence to support the fact that biblical meditation will activate positive long-term changes in both the executive and emotional brain regions. Those who continuously practice meditation on a daily basis appear to have thicker cerebral cortexes than non-meditators. Meditators have increased grey matter in the insula, inferior temporal lobe, frontal lobe, and the hippocampus (see Chapter 1) (Newberg, et al., 2010).

Think of your thalamic region as the primary transportation hub of your brain. Information is sent to the thalamic region for sorting and accurate relaying to the appropriate areas for processing. Blood flow to this region means more efficient functioning. Think about it this way: imagine your local 911 operator not doing their jobs correctly because of faulty phone lines;

think of what that might mean to someone in danger. Now imagine the flip side of that: your local 911 operators are incredibly efficient at their work because they are well-equipped with the necessary tools to do their job. In the first scenario, the faulty phone line is like limited blood flow to the thalamic region; on the other hand, the efficient operator is like a thalamic region with increasing blood flow. This is what meditation does to our brain; it increases blood flow to the thalamic region, thus aiding in the efficiency of information sorting and dissemination to the appropriate brain area for processing.

We know from well-documented research that psychological distress negatively impacts the efficient functioning of the prefrontal cortex. Mental distress causes a reduction in the prefrontal cortex volume, under-developing prefrontal cortex, thus impairing the operation of the prefrontal cortex. The fact that meditation increases blood flow to the prefrontal cortex gives our brains hope of recovery from the damages of psychological distress.

Biblical Meditation and the Frontal-Parietal Circuit

An essential component of biblical meditation is text recitation. There is research demonstrating that bible text recitation activates the frontal-parietal circuit. This circuit includes dorsolateral prefrontal cortex, dorsomedial prefrontal, and medial parietal cortex.

These areas can be significantly damaged by trauma and it's off-shoot of anxiety, depression, and substance abuse. Research indicates that Christian beliefs and practices such as biblical meditation, prayer, and reading of the Bible, increases activity in the frontal-parietal circuit, that is, it increases blood flow in the dorsolateral prefrontal cortex, and ventromedial prefrontal cortex.

This is particularly true if you believe in a loving, caring, kind, compassionate, and faithful God. Thus, an effective way to reduce the impacts of mental disorders is to develop a consistent practice of biblical meditation. This will alleviate the debilitating symptoms associated with anxiety disorders and mood disorders. It also aids in reducing the negative effects that are linked to crisis situations, such as the loss of a family member, health crisis or professional crisis (Dookie, 2017).

Biblical Meditation and Orbitofrontal Cortex

Biblical meditation facilitates the healing of the brain by stimulating neuroplasticity in the grey matter within the orbitofrontal cortex. This is vital to excellent mental health because the orbitofrontal cortex is responsible for emotional regulation, conflict resolution and decision making. Think of someone who is struggling with substance abuse disorders; their ability to choose not to use the substance halted due to the expected perceived reward of the substance. This is where biblical meditation comes in.

It improves the functionality of the orbitofrontal cortex, hence, increases the possibility of making the correct choice not to use the substance.

Meditators have an increase in the cortical thickness in the middle and superior frontal gyrus of their brains. This is like a "no go" switch in the brain; it enables you to improve impulse control and risk aversions. Individuals with impairment in this area of the brain showed reduced activity; however, biblical meditation increases grey matter and activity in the superior frontal gyrus, thus reducing risky behaviors (Dookie, 2017).

Biblical Meditation and Thalamus

Biblical meditation increases grey matter within the thalamus and hypothalamus. The thalamus is responsible for receiving, processing, and distributing sensory information. The thalamus is like a sorting facility of the brain; it determines what information goes to which distinction in the brain. Psychological disorders often times disrupt the effective functioning of the thalamus. Can you imagine that certain vital information needs to get to the brain and due to a disruption in the thalamus, there is a delay in relaying the message. For example, when that body experiences stress and the stressful stimulus has abated, it is the thalamus working in conjunction with the hypothalamus and hippocampus that sends a message to the frontal cortex to inform the system that the stress has abated.

This is where biblical meditation can be effective because the increase in grey matter in the thalamus makes it function as it should (Dookie, 2017).

Biblical Meditation and the Dorsolateral Prefrontal Cortex

The dorsolateral prefrontal cortex is what I called the Christian's weapon against temptations.It fuctions to increse the effort to resist tempations. Evidence has shown that individuals with impairment in this brain area tend to heed to temptation easier than those who have no impairments. Say you are presented with a risky opportunity; it is the dosolateal prefrontal cortex that helps overide the temptation. There are four areas that the dosolateral prefrontal cortex aids: risk taking, controlling urges, inhibitory functioning and effective decision making. Individuals with psychological disorders often have impairments in risk taking, inpulse control, inhibitory functioning, and decision making. Daily biblical meditaion will improve the functioning of the prefrontal cortex. This will improve our ability to make healthy decisions, evaluate risk more effectivly, control imlulses and improve inhibitory functions (Dookie, 2017).

Biblical Meditation and Brain-Derived Neurotrophic Factors

A significant contributing factor to neuroplasticity is a protein called Brain-Derived Neurotrophic Factor (BDNF). It is essential to the survival of neurons by stimulating growth, maturation, and maintenance of neurons. Brain-derived neurotrophic factor is active between the synapses of neurons. The synapses (gap between two neurons), is where neuronal communication takes place. The diagram below illustrates synaptic connectivity; it is between the synapses that BDNF works to stimulate neuroplasticity.

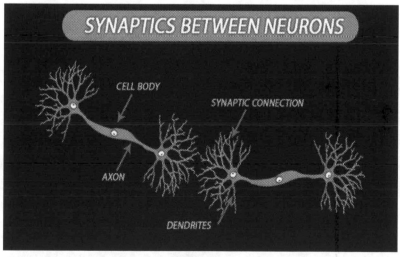

Fig. 1.10

Throughout our life-span, we have different experiences - good, bad and everything in-between; these experiences cause the synapses to change and adapt.

This ability to modify and adapt is known as synaptic plasticity. Brain-Derived Neurotrophic Factor proteins are pivotal to the regulation of synaptic plasticity. This is crucial for memory, encoding, consolidation, and retrieval. Meditation increases the production of BDNF proteins in the anterior cingulate cortex, lateral ventral cortex, prefrontal cortex, orbitofrontal cortex, and the limbic regions. These brain areas are pivotal for cognitive and emotional function.

Early adverse childhood experiences negatively impact the brain's structures, neural circuits, neurotransmitters, and neuropeptides. These experiences activate the fight or flight system (HPA-axis), and create a decrease in GABA-A, noradrenergic, and glucocorticoid receptors. There is a decrease in neuronal migration, myelination, and neurogenesis. It reduces dendritic spines and grey matter in the brain. This is why it is so fascinating to know that God has placed in our brains the ability to heal itself through the process of neuroplasticity. Think of the BDNF as the fertilization that stimulates growth in brain areas that have been damaged by psychological distress. But think of meditation as the substance that makes the fertilization active, in other words, meditation activates the production of the brain-derived neurotrophic factor (Dookie, 2017).

Think of the options of drinking water or juice, of saving or spending, of buying a blue dress or a pink dress, or the choice of going to church or not going to church.

As we progress through a day, we compare reward values of different objects in our environment, and this aids us in making a choice. The part of the brain that is responsible for us having a preference is the orbitofrontal cortex. When this brain area is damaged due to psychological distress, we tend to make inappropriate decisions because of our perception of rewards based on our experience.

I remember working with a young lady who told me that the first time she experienced happiness in her life was when she used cocaine. She then became dependent on cocaine for her happiness. The young lady was severely abused by her father, and then, at the age of fifteen, she was raped by her father's best friend; so, the girl's idea of what gives reward in her environment was thwarted. However, the good news is that meditation practiced on a consistent basis will increase activity in the orbitofrontal cortex. This will activate BDNF protein, thus leading to the plasticity of neurons that have been atrophied due to trauma.

CHAPTER 11

MEDITATION AND THE HEALING OF THE PSYCHOLOGICAL FACULTY

There is a network in the brain known as the default mode network, a system that is implicated in mind-wandering, attention lapse, anxiety, and attention-deficit hyperactivity disorder (ADHD). The areas of the brain that are involved in the activation default mode network are medial, prefrontal and posterior cingulate cortices, dorsal anterior cingulate, and dorsolateral prefrontal cortex. Meditation both decreases the activity of the default mode network and promotes stronger connectivity between respective brain areas.

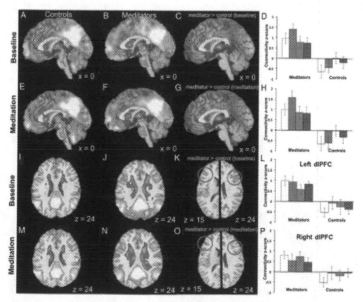

Fig. 1.11

Dr. Courtney Dookie

Adapted from "Meditation experience is associated with differences in default mode network activity and connectivity," by Brewer, Judson A; Worhunsky, Patrick D; Grey, Jeremy R; Tang, Yi-Yuan; Weber, Jochen; Kober, Hedy, 2011. PNAS, p 20254-20259. Copyright 2011 by PNAS

Religious activities such as meditation and prayer will activate the posterior cingulate cortex, dorsal anterior cingulate cortex, and the dorsolateral prefrontal cortex at baseline. The above diagram indicated that the meditator's brain is more active positively both during meditation and baseline in comparison to non-meditators, as opposed to being negatively active due to an overactive default mode network.

Biblical Meditation Heals the Brainstem

Development trauma reduces grey matter in the brain stem. It is a known fact that the brain organizes from bottom to the top. That is, from the brainstem to the cortical areas. The brainstem is implicated in the survival mechanism. Psychological distress alters the development and functionality of the brainstem. The brainstem is responsible for breathing, swallowing, heart rate, blood pressure, consciousness, and being awake or asleep. That is the reason individuals with trauma history tend to have irregular heartbeats, breathing problems, blood pressure irregularities, and problems with sleep and awake time.

The primary psychological function of the brainstem is that it houses anxiety or arousal states that are associated with the experience of the trauma; this contributes to the persistent "state of fear" that individuals with trauma history experience. It is the first brain area to be damaged by trauma.

Recent research reports that meditation increases grey matter in the brainstem. This means that religious contemplation activates neuroplasticity in the brainstem; this will positively impact the function and structure of the brainstem. The brainstem structure includes the pons, locus coeruleus, reticular formation, nucleus raphe, and sensory trimentum nucleus (Dookie, 2017). Another way to bring calmness to the brainstem is through rhythm. Contemplation and participation in Christian musical rhythm can aid in regulating the brainstem. This includes singing, playing instruments, and dancing. The Bible tells us that rhythm was an important part of God's people's lives.

Psalm 149:3- Let them praise his name with dancing, making melody to him with tambourine and lyre!

Psalm 150:4- Praise him with tambourine and dance; praise him with strings and pipe!

Psalm 30:11-You have turned for me my mourning into dancing; you have loosed my sackcloth and clothed me with gladness.

Psalm 66:1-To the choirmaster. A Song. A Psalm. Shout for joy to God, all the earth;

Psalm 33:3-Sing to him a new song; play skillfully on the strings, with loud shouts.

Psalm 95:1-Oh come, let us sing to the Lord; let us make a joyful noise to the rock of our salvation!

Exodus 15:20- Then Miriam the prophetess, the sister of Aaron, took a tambourine in her hand, and all the women went out after her with tambourines and dancing.

Psalm 150:1-6- Praise the Lord! Praise God in his sanctuary; praise him in his mighty heavens! Praise him for his mighty deeds; praise him according to his excellent greatness! Praise him with trumpet sound; praise him with lute and harp! Praise him with tambourine and dance; praise him with strings and pipe! Praise him with sounding cymbals; praise him with loud clashing cymbals!

Notice in the above verses, the combination of singing, dancing, and the playing of musical instruments. The essential theme here is rhythm. Rhythm aids in regulating the brainstem; thus, regulating our emotions. Therefore, make music a part of your lives, and it will promote peak psychological health in your life.

Keisha, 27-years-old, came into my office. She had been emotionally and physically abused by her mother and started to use drugs at age 13 to manage her feelings.

She ran away from home at age 14 and had been living on her own since. Keisha was raped three times and physically abused by two familiar partners. She cried regularly and found it difficult to be alone. When she came to see me, she told me that she started to attend church and one of the ladies said she should seek therapy. She was then introduced to Christian instrumental and Christian music. She stated that the music helped her to sleep and manage her feelings. It is clear from Keisha's experience that music regulates her sleep cycle and her emotions. Since starting to listen to music daily, she is less heightened and cries less. This is indicative of the positive impact of rhythm on the brain, which includes the brainstem.

Biblical Meditation Heals the Limbic System

Moving from the brainstem, which is the first level of the brain house, we move into the second level or mid-brain; this is also referred to as the limbic system or emotional brain. Psychological distress can severely damage the structures of the limbic system, and the limbic brain area is the most implicated in psychological distress. The limbic system is a network of interconnected brain structures. These include the hippocampus, limbic cortex, sections of the hypothalamus, anterior thalamic nuclei, and the amygdala.

Mental distress increases the amygdala volume and reactivity, resulting in limbic irritability.

Chronic stress causes the release of glucocorticoid, which leads to the remodeling and inhibition of cell proliferation in the prefrontal cortex and the hippocampus. Glucocorticoid causes an increase in the spread of neuronal growth and dendritic in the amygdala, making it difficult to regulate fear and anxiety (Dookie, 2017).

The hippocampus is responsible for memory encoding and retrieval. The amygdala is the brain's alarm to inform the brain that something is wrong. Psychological distress leads to an increase in the amygdala hyper-responsive and reactive process. There is an increase in the amygdala size due to trauma. The amygdala and the hippocampus work close to each other; that is the reason emotional memory is so strong. Every time the amygdala is triggered, the hippocampus attaches significance to the experience, thus, emotional memory is created. This is the reason veterans can be triggered by the backfiring of a car muffler when they return home. Being in the combat zone, their brain attaches significance to the sound of blasts, bombs, and gun fire; thus, similar sounds in a non-threating environment will trigger their memories of the experience. Being regularly exposed to emotionally charged situations for long periods of time will eventually reduce the hippocampal volume and lower the grey matter concentration (Dookie, 2017).

The activation of the amygdala due to trauma or other psychological distress leads to the activation of the sympathetic nervous system.

The activation of the sympathetic nervous system activates our white blood cells (known as macrophages-big eaters). The white blood cells release cytokines, which function like scattered bullets in our body. When this process continues for extended periods of time because of psychological distress, it damages the insulin receptors and glucocorticoids receptors; it interferes with the following neurotransmitters: norepinephrine, serotonin, dopamine, and other neurochemicals. This results in increased diabetes, obesity, high blood cholesterol, stroke, autoimmune problems, and bone density loss (Dookie, 2017).

Impairment in the limbic system is linked to anxiety, depression, post-traumatic stress disorder, developmental trauma disorder, borderline personality disorder, disruptive mood dysregulation disorder, anger, irritability, and suicidal tendencies. Meditation can be used to treat the brain following psychological distress. The brain areas that undergo plasticity in the limbic system due to meditation are hippocampus, amygdala, and hypothalamic. There is evidence supporting the fact that meditation activates the parasympathetic nervous system, thus, aiding in the regulation of the body's responses to emotional distress.

Imagine that: thinking about the love of God can change the structure and function of your brain through the process of neuroplasticity. Wow! Biblical meditation initiates neuroplasticity in the limbic system.

This will improve emotional regulation, aiding in the recovery from anxiety, depression, post-traumatic stress disorder, developmental trauma disorder, borderline personality disorder, disruptive mood dysregulation disorder, anger, irritability, and suicidality (Dookie, 2017).

Biblical Meditation Heals the Cortical Brain Structures

The cortical brain in the third level of the brain house is the part of the brain responsible for executive functions. The executive role takes into account both the emotional and rational functioning of the brain. Psychological distress leads to the reduction in the frontal cortex volume. Mood disorders severely impact the prefrontal cortex. The prefrontal cortex functions to regulate mood, attention, and immune functions. Mood disorders lower activity and blood flow to the prefrontal cortex. Areas of the cortical brain include prefrontal cortex, ventromedial prefrontal cortex, dorsolateral prefrontal cortex, anterior cingulate cortex, and orbitofrontal cortex (Dookie, 2017).

Before looking at how psychological distress impacts the above cortical brain areas, let's look at the case of John. John is 55 years old. He grew up in a home with very conservative Christian parents. He was told that if he did not behave himself in a holy and righteous manner, he would be damned to hell and burn forever. John's picture of God was that He is a punitive and angry God.

He is always angry with humans for not obeying Him. John is a successful computer programmer, and two years ago, John failed his managerial exam three times by two points, one point, and 1.5 points respectively. He concluded that he was good for nothing and that God was punishing him for getting married to a non-Christian woman. John stopped going to work. He spends most of his time in his room playing video games. He does not enjoy being around people, and he finds no pleasure in life anymore. John was diagnosed with major depression disorder (Dookie, 2017).

The prefrontal cortex regulates behavior, thought, and emotion via a top-down regulatory mechanism. It is essential for providing flexible, goal-directed behavior, such as the ability to inhibit inappropriate impulses, regulation of attention, reality testing, and insight about one's own and others' actions. An individual who experiences psychological distress often finds it difficult to concentrate, to establish goals, and to control attention. Their perception of reality is often impaired. Psychological distress reduces the grey matter in the prefrontal cortex, weakens prefrontal cortex functional connectivity, and prefrontal cortex regulation of the amygdala. One way to think about functional connectivity is the decoupling of different brain regions. This means that there is a reduction in cerebral blood flow (Dookie, 2017).

The orbital and ventromedial prefrontal cortex functions to regulate emotion. Dysfunction in the ventromedial prefrontal cortex is fundamental to the development of mood and anxiety disorders. It is a crucial component of our social and emotional functioning, thus when impaired by psychological distress, this leads to challenges in social and emotional functioning. The reason for this is due to the connection between the ventromedial prefrontal cortex and the amygdala. Research indicates that functional reduction of the ventromedial prefrontal cortex causes heightened amygdala activity. In individuals who suffer from psychological disorders, the ventromedial prefrontal cortex tends to be overactive (Dookie, 2017).

The dorsolateral prefrontal cortex is responsible for the cognitive control emotions. It is vital in controlling the physical pain perception and, to a lesser extent, psychological pain. There is research indicating that a large percentage of people who visit their family physician for physical pain are told that their physical pain is a result of psychological distress. In my own practice, I have recognized that a number of clients diagnosed with psychological disorders often suffer from physical pain (Dookie, 2017).

Dysfunction in the dorsolateral prefrontal cortex is linked to major depression. Psychological distress causes suppression in the dorsolateral prefrontal cortex; this is the reason it is difficult to make a practical decision when an individual is suffering from a psychological disorder.

This is caused by the individual's behavior, especially the ones who are reinforced due to the experience of rewards. The orbital-prefrontal cortex is central to the reinforcement of reward-related behaviors. Mental illness suppresses the activity of the orbital prefrontal cortex. This is especially salient for approach-avoidant behaviors.

Along with the anterior cingulate cortex, the orbital prefrontal cortex is essential for conflict resolution. Often the inappropriate display of anger is a direct result of suppressed or damaged orbital prefrontal cortex because the orbital prefrontal cortex is connected to the reinforcement of reward-related behaviors; it is also strongly associated with addictive behaviors; this includes both substance and process addictions. In recent brain research, responses such as excessive swearing, addictions, hypersexuality, and low social skills are linked to damage in the orbital prefrontal cortex (Dookie, 2017).

Given the extensive negative impact of psychological distress on the cortical brain areas, it is no wonder that it takes an intervention from God to bring healing to our lives and the lives of those who have experienced the claws of mental disorders. Did you know that having a healthy religious belief system about God and ourselves increases blood flow to the various areas of the prefrontal cortex? Regions such as the ventromedial prefrontal cortex (VMPFC) and dorsolateral prefrontal cortex (DLPFC)?

Meditation and prayer increase activity and grey matter in the frontal lobe, dorsolateral prefrontal cortex, ventromedial prefrontal cortex and the anterior cingulate cortex. Biblical meditation facilitates neuroplasticity in the frontal lobe, dorsolateral prefrontal cortex, ventromedial prefrontal cortex, and the anterior cingulate cortex. Reciting and meditating on biblical texts increases the activity in the frontal-parietal circuit. There are recent findings that support the fact that the ventral medial prefrontal cortex (VMPFC), dorsolateral prefrontal cortex (DLPFC), hippocampus, para hippocampal gyrus, middle temporal gyrus, temporal pole, and retrosplenial cortex are more active in individuals who practice meditation on a daily basis. Since meditation triggers the brain's ability to initiate the process of neurogenesis, this activates neuroplasticity in the above brain areas. This gives individuals who have experienced trauma or have challenges with mental disorders the opportunity of receiving the healing that God intended. Can you imagine just spending time with God can bring healing to our lives?

Biblical Meditation Regulates Neurotransmitters

In the last two decades, there has been a plethora of research examining the impact of psychological distress on the brain. You have seen above the effect of trauma and mental suffering on the physical structure of the brain. In this section, I will discuss the impact of psychological distress on the neurochemicals in the brain. These neurochemicals are called neurotransmitters. The following neurotransmitters are implicated in psychological distress: serotonin, dopamine, norepinephrine, gamma-aminobutyric acid (GABA) and glutamate (Dookie, 2017).

Norepinephrine

Think of a time when you were fearful or scared. You remember how your heart beat faster, the palms of your hands started to sweat, and your pupils began to dilate? These are a result of the release or increase of norepinephrine in your body. It is released from the sympathetic nervous system in response to stress. In psychological distress, such as developmental trauma, stress, attention deficit hyperactivity disorder, and anxiety, there is an increased level of norepinephrine. This is associated with the impaired ability to think coherently, panic attacks, impending sense of doom, hyperarousal, and restlessness in the body and mind.

On the other hand, studies indicate that depression is associated with an abnormality in norepinephrine. Norepinephrine works along the noradrenergic pathways in the brain. This pathway runs from the locus coeruleus to the various regions of the cerebral and the spinal cord. It also projects to the limbic system, thus impacting emotional regulation and cognitive functioning. This is the reason individuals who are affected by depression have challenges with appetite, response to pain, levels of pleasure, sexual satisfaction, and aggressive behaviors (Dookie, 2017).

Numerous studies are indicating that individuals who meditate have lower levels of norepinephrine released into the brain. This is good news for individuals who experience trauma and who suffer from anxiety. The practice of biblical meditation can lower norepinephrine in the body; this will aid in managing the symptoms associated with depression, anxiety, attention deficit hyperactive disorder, and developmental trauma disorder.

Serotonin

This neurotransmitter plays a vital role in mood regulation and control. Whenever there is a deficiency of serotonin, it is correlated with an increase in depressive systems. An imbalance of serotonin, norepinephrine, and dopamine is associated with depression.

Serotonin is linked to the regulation of mood, sleep, aggression, eating, and sexual behavior, and all these functions are impacted by depression. Serotonin is also connected to anxiety disorder. An imbalance in serotonin often results in excessive worrying, rumination, difficulty controlling emotions and impulses, and hypersensitivity (Dookie, 2017).

Several studies have shown that meditation increases the production of serotonin and an increase in serotonin is associated with positive effects. In other words, the right balance of serotonin in the brain aids in alleviating the symptomologies of depression and anxiety. Meditation activates the dorsal raphe via stimulation of lateral hypothalamic area, thus increasing serotonin levels. An increase in serotonin levels was demonstrated by testing urine samples of individuals after meditation.

Dopamine

Dopamine is connected to several mental illnesses, such as mood disorders, attention deficit/hyperactive disorder, anxiety, and schizophrenia. The following symptoms are related to the imbalance in dopamine: inability to feel pleasure, loss of motivation, delusions/psychosis, and obsession with details. Meditation activates the dopaminergic system via the basal ganglia, leading to a 65% increase of dopamine in the brain (Dookie, 2017).

Meditation also increases the levels of the following amino-acids: glutamate and gamma-aminobutyric acid (GABA). The increase in glutamate is a result of increased activity in the prefrontal cortex due to meditation. Psychological disorders such as personality disorders and social disorders are also connected to an imbalance in both neurotransmitters and amino acids. Drug and alcohol use is linked to GABA receptors. GABA functions to slow the speed of nerve impulses and causes muscles to relax (Dookie, 2017).

Neuroplasticity is activated by meditative practice to bring healing to the different areas of the brain that have been damaged by depression, anxiety, developmental trauma disorders, attention deficit/hyperactive disorder and other psychological distresses. Meditation is one way to apply neuroplasticity in adults who have experienced psychological distress clinically. Meditation and intense prayer trigger the brain's ability to initiate the neurogenesis process. Those who believe in the essence of their meditative practice get more benefits from the exercise. Christian beliefs and practices increase activity in the dorsolateral prefrontal cortex (Dookie, 2017).

Meditation increases activities in the ACC and increases white matter. The hippocampus, which is crucial for memory encoding and retrieval, is an area of the brain that is negatively impacted by mental illnesses. Research indicates that meditation facilitates neuroplasticity in the hippocampus.

The hippocampus' structure is more substantial in individuals who practice meditation in comparison to those who do not practice meditation.

Let us look at a summary of the positive impacts of biblical meditation (BM) on the brain:

1. 1.   BM increase CBF to Frontal lobe and thalamic region
2. BM activates long-term changes in the cortical and subcortical brain areas
3. BM increase grey matter in the insula inferior temporal lobe, frontal lobe, hippocampus

4. BM (text recitation) increase activities in the DLFC, VMPFC, ACC, Basal ganglia
5. BM increase neuroplasticity in grey matter, cell bodies, dendrites, axon terminal of neurons.
6. BM meditation increased grey matter within the thalamus, dorsolateral prefrontal cortex
7. BM increased the production of plasma level of BDNF
8. BM increase grey matter in brainstem (pons, reticular formation)
9. BM activate neuroplasticity in the hippocampus, amygdala, hypothalamus
10. BM enables the Parasympathetic Nervous system
11. BM activates the dopamine system, increases serotonin, and increases amino-acids, GABA.

From the preceding, it is clear that biblical meditation can aid in balancing the neurochemicals, and restructure and create new pathways in our brain; this, in turn, helps to heal the mind from psychological distress.

CHAPTER 12

MEDITATION AND THE HEALING OF THE RELATIONAL FACULTY

In the gospel of Matthew 22:36-40, we have this encounter with Jesus. One of the leaders of Judaism came to Him and said, "Teacher, which is the greatest commandment in the Law? Jesus replied: "Love the Lord your God with all your heart, and with all your soul and with all your mind." This is the first and greatest commandment. And the second is like it: 'Love your neighbor as yourself. 'All the Law and the Prophets hang on these two commandments.'"

Noticed Jesus' answer; it incorporates a duality of relationships. The first relationship is between God and humanity. This relationship will be explored in the next chapter. The second relationship Jesus mentioned in the above passage is the interpersonal relationship; this relationship exists between humans. From the moment we are conceived in our mother's womb, we initiate the process of being wired for relationships, and our brains are wired for these connections.

We live in a society that promotes individuality over interconnectivity. Due to this, we have more people who are suffering from loneliness, self-centeredness, and a range of mental disorders that are rooted in broken relationships.

God intended that we should flourish and create lasting bonds. The ten commandments are centered on forming the correct bonds. The first four commandments point to a relationship with God, and the last six points to a relationship with each other.

Neurobiology of Interpersonal Relationship

The brain is shaped and organized based on the relationship system between caregivers and children. As mentioned in the chapter on insecure attachment, numerous brain structures and functions have been disrupted by insecure attachment. In this chapter, we are going to explore how healthy interpersonal relationships can heal the brain.

The experiences we have in our environments shape the brain structures and influence its functionality throughout the life-span, and healthy relationships activate the neurons in our brains. The experience of a healthy relationship shapes, or you may say re-shapes, the function of neural activity. Take for example someone who has experienced insecure attachment in early relationships; their brain would have undergone some severely harmful structural and functional damages. Fast forward to this same person in the future - now they are in a healthy relationship. The healthy relationship they enter into later in life will stimulate the process of neurogenesis in the brain.

The process of neurogenesis will initiate the process of neuroplasticity. Thus, a healthy interpersonal relationship later in life can correct damages caused by an insecure attachment in childhood (Perry, Riege, & Brown, 1999; van der Kolk, The neurobiolology of childhood trauma and abuse, 2003).

Biblical Meditation and Interpersonal Relationships

There are two types of biblical meditation that can improve interpersonal relationships. These meditations are compassion and loving-kindness meditation.

Compassion

In defining compassion, researchers have done a meta-analysis of compassion. They proposed a definition that encompasses five components. These components are recognition of suffering, understanding its universality, concerns for those who are suffering, tolerating the distress associated with the witnessing of pain, and the motivation to act or take action to alleviate the suffering. These components are the desire or the awareness to ease the suffering of others and the willingness to alleviate the sufferings of humanity. It is the essential teaching of Christianity. Recall the following passage in the book of Matthew 25: 31-40

> [31] "When the Son of Man comes in His glory, and all the holy angels with Him, then He will sit on the throne of His glory. [32] All the nations will be gathered before Him, and He will separate them one from another, as a shepherd divides his sheep from the goats. [33] And He will set the sheep on His right hand, but the goats on the left. [34] Then the King will say to those on His right hand, 'Come, you blessed of My Father, inherit the kingdom prepared for you from the foundation of the world: [35] for I was hungry, and you gave Me food; I was thirsty, and you gave Me drink. I was a stranger, and you took Me in; [36] I was naked, and you clothed Me; I was sick, and you visited Me; I was in prison, and you came to Me."

> [37] "Then the righteous will answer Him, saying, 'Lord, when did we see You hungry and feed You, or thirsty and give You drink? [38] When did we see You a stranger and take You in, or naked and clothe You? [39] Or when did we see You sick, or in prison, and come to You?' [40] And the King will answer and say to them, 'Assuredly, I say to you, inasmuch as you did it to one of the least of these My brethren, you did it to Me.'

In this passage, you will have recognized that Jesus' primary lesson to his followers was that they needed to act in alleviating the sufferings of those who are naked, thirsty, hungry, strangers, sick, and in prison. Can you imagine what the world would be like if we all develop compassion for each other? Talk about a piece of heaven on earth; that is what it would be like because we would initiate a deep internal desire to ease the sufferings of others. In compassion meditation, the practitioner moves from a self-oriented perspective to other-oriented perspective.

The meditator begins by visualizing how, and what it would be like, to aid in alleviating the pains that the human family is experiencing. Based on neuroimaging studies, in doing so, the insula and the anterior cingulate cortices will activate because of the compassionate response to the suffering of the other person(s). The research indicates that our willingness to have compassion for others will improve our empathic reaction to social stimuli.

As I mentioned earlier, compassionate meditation activates the anterior cingulate cortex and the insula cortex. The activation of the insula cortex aids in monitoring the body's internal homeostasis. The desire to alleviate the suffering of others will give the insula cortex and the anterior cingulate cortex the functional capacity to detect emotions and map their physiological symptoms within the body and communicate this information to the other parts of the brain. This allows us to feel what others are experiencing, not on a superficial level, but in a more profound sense. We become more emotionally attuned with ourselves and others.

The anterior cingulate cortex functions in deciding what gets attention, monitoring conflicts, making choices, and making decisions. Similar to insula, the anterior cingulate cortex will alert other brain regions to the need for increased cognitive control to resolve conflicts, to make a choice, and to make decisions. I want you to envision the broader implications of the functions of the anterior cingulate cortex. Picture what it would be like for us to have compassion for others, unselfish compassion. It would allow us to care for the needs of others, but we would reap the byproduct of paying attention to others, which would increase cognitive and emotional control. Note, we are not doing it because we want to improve emotional and cognitive control, but to help in caring for others.

Loving-Kindness

Another type of meditation that has profound biblical significance is loving-kindness meditation. The Loving-kindness meditation is fundamentally rooted in the principle of love for all humanity. The Bible refers to this kind of love as unconditional love or agape love. It is given without any expectation of it being reciprocated, and it is not limited to friends or family. In the Christian framework, this type of love has three dimensions: love of God, love of self, and love of others. This kind of love is summed up in Luke 10:27 - "'Love the Lord your God with all your heart and with all your soul and with all your strength and with all your mind'; and, 'Love your neighbor as yourself.'"

There are seven phases of loving-kindness meditation: (1) Attention to God. (2) Attention to the self; this does not mean selfishness and self-centeredness. It is love for the self through the eyes of God. (3) Attention to family. (4) Attention to close friends. (5) Attention to neutral people. (6) Attention to enemies. (7) Attention or focus on community/ and the universe. Notice that it starts with God and ends with the universe, an equal connectedness - a connection to God and connection to the universe (Lippelt, Hommel, & Colzato, 2014).

Research indicates that loving-kindness meditation improves social connections and positivity towards others. It increases your positive emotional experiences, and it generates a positive emotional experience that can extend to your daily life and reshape your personality traits. Practicing loving-kindness meditation will improve your social connection, in that your perception of others and yourself with others will begin to take a positive perspective. This will significantly help with individuals who suffer from social anxiety or individuals who experience difficulties with social interactions (Lippelt, Hommel, & Colzato, 2014).

Loving-kindness meditation has been shown to increase grey matter volume in our brain, especially areas of the brain that specialize in emotional regulation. Like compassionate meditation, loving-kindness meditation activates the insula and the anterior cingulate cortex and aids in cognitive control. Emotional regulation enhances positive emotions and reduces negative emotions.

Loving-kindness meditation and compassionate meditation allow us to change our perception of ourselves and others. If you desire to increase love, empathy, and compassion for self, and other, I recommend, to begin with, practicing some loving-kindness meditation and compassionate meditation. Some research supports the validity that loving-kindness and compassionate meditation brings healing from shame, guilt, self-criticism, anxiety, anger, sadness, hopelessness, and disgust. There is also research indicating that loving-kindness and compassionate meditation soothe negative auditory voices associated with schizophrenia (Lippelt, Hommel, & Colzato, 2014).

So, do you need to improve your connectedness, both to God and humanity? Are you suffering from social anxiety or other forms of social impairment? Then now is the time to engage in compassion for self and others through the eyes of God.

13

MEDITATION AND THE HEALING OF THE SPIRITUAL FACULTY

Biblical meditation is thoughtful focusing of attention on God's word through scripture, His character of love, morality, and compassion, and using silence or vocalization to produce positive impacts on the practitioner's thoughts, feelings, and actions. The data indicates that those who believe in a loving, compassionate, caring, and faithful God are at an advantage over those who do not believe in God. This is particularly evident in the healing from complex trauma via the process of neuroplasticity.

The contemplation of the character of God will result in a larger hippocampus structure. Worshiping God plays a vital role in rebuilding the brain's neural pathways. The brain areas of the hippocampus, Para hippocampal gyrus, middle temporal gyrus, temporal pole, and frontal cortex are more active in individuals who have an intensely intimate relationship with God than those who do not believe in God. Having daily worship in which we focus our attention on God will activate the anterior cingulate cortex (ACC) and dorsolateral prefrontal cortex.

Personal Worship and Brain healing

Worshiping God through the process of focused attention and open monitoring will reshape brain structures, neural circuits, neurotransmitter systems, and neuropeptide systems. The contemplation of God will improve dendritic spins, grey matter in the brain, brain stem regulation, limbic system structures, and cortical brain structures.

You can increase your neuronal migration, myelination, and neurogenesis through daily worship. Building a personal relationship with God will activate the parasympathetic nervous system in the brain and the body to a place of rest, thus, leading to the deactivation of the sympathetic nervous system. This will deactivate the HPA-axis. In turn, there will be a reduction in the symptoms associated with mental disorders, such as anxiety, depression, developmental trauma disorder, and dissociation.

The Bible tells us to worship God in spirit and in truth. The truth is that God loves you with an everlasting love; God loves you when you do not love yourself, and God loves you before you even consider loving him. Worshiping this wonderful God of love will increase grey matter in the brain stem; this is an area of the brain that receives extensive damage due to trauma or other forms of psychological distress. Worshiping the God of love will lead to positive changes in both the limbic system and the emotional center of the brain. The brain areas that undergo plasticity in the limbic system due to worship are the hippocampus-amygdala and hypothalamic.

No wonder Jesus said to us "Come unto all you who are weary and heavy-laden with burdens of pain, suffering, and sadness and I will give you the peace that brings healing and restoration." In Isaiah 53, the prophet declares to us that Jesus has borne our griefs, our sorrows, our afflictions, and that we are healed by his suffering. Spending time with Jesus in worship will allow us to focus on his love when he died on the cross for us. Spending time with God in prayer will enable us to develop a healthy relationship with Him; this will activate the neurogenesis process in our brains.

Given the negative repercussions of developmental trauma and other psychological distress, having a healthy belief system in God will stimulate the healing process. Evidence suggests that spirituality plays a crucial role in rebuilding the brain's neural pathways. The brain areas of the hippocampus, para hippocampal gyrus, middle temporal gyrus, temporal pole, and frontal cortex are more active in individuals who worship God on a consistent and continuous basis compared to those who do not. It also activates the ACC and dorsolateral prefrontal cortex.

A consistent devotional life will activate the dopaminergic system via the basal ganglia, leading to an increase of dopamine in the brain. The way it works is that when we worship the God of love and compassion, it activates the dorsal raphe via stimulation of the lateral hypothalamic area, thus increasing serotonin levels.

Notice that worshiping God stimulates neurochemicals in our brain that are essential for restoring integration in the brain and ultimately the whole system.

In this section, we see the importance of worship in the process of neuroplasticity. The areas of the brain that are taken into account due to prayer and meditation are the cortical, which includes the frontal, temporal, and parietal lobe; the subcortical or limbic system, which consists of the amygdala, thalamus, hippocampus, hypothalamus, and basal ganglia; and the brain stem, which includes the reticular formation, pons, medulla, locus coeruleus, nucleus raphe, and sensory triennium nucleus. The data was also analyzed to elucidate the impact of meditation on different neurochemicals, namely, dopamine, serotonin, GABA, glutamate, and melatonin. All of these brain structures and brain chemicals that meditation impacts are directly related to the process of neuroplasticity.

CHAPTER 14

BIBLICAL MEDITATIVE TECHNIQUES

In the seminars that I have done, a common question that I often hear is, how do we practice biblical meditation? In previous chapters I have touched on various techniques of biblical meditation; if you missed it, in this section, I will define six techniques that I recommend when practicing biblical meditation. These six techniques are also used in other forms of meditation.

Biblical focused attention meditation

In this meditative practice, the practitioner allows his or her mind to focus on a chosen object or event (Lippelt, Hommel, & Colzato, 2014). In biblical meditation, the object of meditation is on God and His actions in the life of humanity. The meditator would turn his or her mind to God; this is done by reading the scriptures and permitting the mind to be saturated with the events of the scriptures and how those events can be applied to our daily lives.

Biblical open monitoring meditation

In open monitoring meditation, the practitioners become aware of themselves, specifically their thoughts and emotions, without judging (Lippelt, Hommel, & Colzato, 2014). As meditators become open to the themes of the bible, they will experience various emotions and thoughts. In the open monitoring technique, the practitioner will <u>not immediately</u> try to change his or her thoughts or feelings; he or she would just observe them from a non-judgmental perspective (Dookie, 2017).

Biblical loving-kindness meditation

In biblical loving kindness meditation, the practitioner incorporates principles from both focus attention and open monitoring meditation (Lippelt, Hommel, & Colzato, 2014). The practitioner focuses on Jesus Christ (object) and the work of love and compassion that He demonstrated towards humanity. In loving kindness meditation, the meditator develops Christ's love and compassion for him or herself, and then extends that love and compassion towards others (Davidson & Lutz, 2008; Dookie, 2017).

Biblical mindfulness meditation

In biblical mindfulness, the practitioner's goal is to develop an awareness of the present moment's experience of perceptible mental process. The practice of biblical mindfulness seeks to engage the mind to pay attention and focus on becoming aware of the present with intention and purpose. In the practice of biblical mindfulness, the individual becomes aware of the self in the present moment and how God is interacting with him or her in that moment.

Christo-centric Music meditation: Rhythm

In previous chapters, it was discussed where most disorders are because of dysregulation and lack of integration in our brain systems. One method that has been used to promote integration in the brain is rhythm. Music is one of the most effective methods to regulating and promoting integration. When Christ-centered music is included into the practice of biblical meditation, this will promote healthy growth in neural pathways and myelination process of brain restoration.

It is important for practitioners to choose songs that center their attention on God and encourage an understanding of His love and compassion, as well as give the meditators an opportunity to purposely reach out to God through focused attention. This is what most worship groups would term as 'praise and worship'. The scripture says, "Speaking to yourselves in psalms and hymns and spiritual songs, singing and making melody in your heart to the Lord" (Ephesians 5:19). It is evident that when dwelling in a meditative experience with God, the worshiper is encouraged to use music and scripture together. Examples of biblical related music are hymns, gospel music, and scripture songs.

Mindfulness Prayer

Prayer involves uttering inner thoughts and yearnings to God. This complements the process of focused attention, which helps the meditator to receive intimate messages from God through the scripture or inspiration. It complements our response in loving kindness meditation where we center our experience with God and reach out to humanity. It complements our being mindful of the present in worship and epitomizes the expression of our reciprocal interaction with God. Prayer is the opening of the heart to God as to a friend (White, 2000). The action of uttering either through whispering or audible conversation, involves breathing and pacing one's self through words uttered.

Readers should be keen to understand that there is mindless prayer and mindful prayer. Mindless prayer excludes a reciprocal connection with God as described above; this can often result in shallow breathing and impaired rhythmic movement of the breath. Mindful prayer means that our minds are drawn out towards God as we connect with His work, mercies, and blessings in our lives. Uttering this experience giving praise and thanksgiving or uttering in repentance and heart searching requires being present in the moment while doing paced utterance to God. In the Jewish culture, it is known as chanting the sacred texts back to God. This process encompasses deep breathing and rhythmic breathing.

When the meditator practices prayer, not only does their mind connect to God, but their brain structure starts to change from a neuronal level. Prayer changes the brain by changing the neurons. This is done by a process called neuroplasticity. The average human brain has approximately 100 billon neurons, each neuron having at least 10,000 connections. That means, there are over 1000 trillion connections in the average human brain. Therefore, by praying, we can change the structure and function of our brain; each neuron is being impacted by communication with God.

This is evident through the testimonies of countless individuals who profess that their lives, which were filled with self-destructive behaviors, were changed through the practice of humble, sincere prayer even after trying everything else, including medication and psychotherapy.

Work Sheets

In this section, I will present four sample worksheets that you can use to practice one version of biblical meditation. These sheets are not exhaustive in themselves, but just an example. The worksheets are the ones I use with clients that I see in my practice who are willing to try the method. What I have observed is that all the clients who try this technique report positive changes. I will organize the worksheets according to different psychological disorders. This does not mean that they are only to be used with the suggested psychological disorder.

These pages are already set up - just follow the procedures in the worksheet for 30 days, twice per day.

To make it dynamic, verses, song lyrics, and songs will change every ten days. You can choose other applicable Bible verses and songs; however, it is recommended that the principle outline is followed. I have included one sample opening prayer; you need not follow this prayer but allow prayer to flow naturally from your heart as if you were talking to a friend. Let's take a look at the samples.

Sample #1: Pornography Addiction

Pornography addiction
Name: Anthony John
Dates: January 18, 2018
Morning Practice: 7 am
Evening Practice: 8 pm

Start with a short prayer:

Example: Lord, thank you for waking me this morning. Open my mind as I seek to worship you. Send your Holy Spirit to guide and teach me your ways and your desires for my life. Give me strength and wisdom from meditating on your Words. In your keep and care, I commit my life, my struggles, and my ultimate victory. In Jesus' Name. Amen.

Two Christian Songs:

Hymns such as:

1. "Take my life and let it be consecrated Lord to Thee."
2. "All to Jesus I surrender, All to Him I freely give" will be appropriate.

Read your Bible

Key Text # 1: 2 Corinthians 10:5

"Casting down arguments and every high thing that exalts itself against the knowledge of God, bringing every thought into captivity to the obedience of Christ."

Key Text #2: Philippians 4:8

"Finally, brethren, whatsoever things are true, whatsoever things are honest, whatsoever things are just, whatsoever things are pure, whatsoever things are lovely, whatsoever things are of good report; if there be any virtue, and if there be any praise, think on these things."

Action Plan: Part A

Memorize/Meditate on the Bible verses

Ask yourself, what does the verse mean to me?

How can you apply it to my life?

Action Plan: Part B: Reflection Time

What was the experience like?

Thoughts   _____

Feelings   _____

Actions   _____

Ending Prayer: In this prayer, you are pouring your heart out to God; let Him know all your thoughts, feelings and desires. Pray His words back to Him. In other words, wrestle with God to apply victory to your life.

Keep reciting this key text throughout the day

"Finally, brethren, whatsoever things are true, whatsoever things are honest, whatsoever things are just, whatsoever things are pure, whatsoever things are lovely, whatsoever things are of good report; if there be any virtue, and if there be any praise, think on these things."

Evening Worship at your desired time: Repeat the process.

<u>Sample #2: Anxiety</u>

Name: Paul
Dates: January 18, 2018
Morning Practice: 7 am
Evening Practice: 8 pm

Start with a short prayer:

Example: Lord, thank you for waking me this morning. Open my mind as I seek to worship you. Send your Holy Spirit to guide and teach me your ways and your desires for my life. Give me strength and wisdom from meditating on your Words. In your keep and care, I commit my life, my struggles, and my ultimate victory. In Jesus' Name. Amen.

Two Christian Songs:

Hymns such as:

1. "Take my life and let it be consecrated Lord to Thee."
2. "All to Jesus I surrender, All to Him I freely give" will be appropriate.

Read your Bible

Key Text: 2 Timothy 1:7

"For God hath not given us the spirit of fear, but of power, and of love, and of a sound mind."

Key Text: 2 Corinthians 1:3-4

"Praise be to the God and father of our Lord Jesus Christ, the father of compassion and the God of all comfort, who comforts us in all troubles so that we can comfort those in any trouble with the comfort we ourselves receive from God."

Action Plan: Part A

Memorize/Meditate on the Bible verses

Ask yourself what does the verse mean to me?

How can you apply it to my life?

Action Plan: Part B: Reflection Time

What was the experience like?

Thoughts _____

Feelings _____

Actions _____

Ending Prayer: In this prayer, you are pouring your heart to God, let Him know all your thoughts, feelings and desires. Pray His words back to Him. In other words, wrestle with God to apply victory to your life.

Keep reciting the key text throughout the day. "For God has not given us the spirit of fear, but of power, and of love, and of a sound mind."

Evening Worship at your desired time: Repeat the process.

Sample #3: Depression

Name: Paul
Dates: January 18, 2018
Morning Practice: 7 am
Evening Practice: 8 pm

Start with a short prayer:

Example: Lord, thank you for waking me this morning. Open my mind as I seek to worship you. Send your Holy Spirit to guide and teach me your ways and your desires for my life. Give me strength and wisdom from meditating on your Words. In your keep and care, I commit my life, my struggles, and my ultimate victory. In Jesus' Name. Amen.

Two Christian Songs:

Hymns such as:

1. "Take my life and let it be consecrated Lord to Thee."
2. "All to Jesus I surrender, All to Him I freely give" will be appropriate.

Read your Bible

Key Text: Psalm 34:18,19

"The LORD is close to the brokenhearted and saves those who are crushed in spirit. (19) A righteous man may have many troubles, but the Lord delivers him from them all."

Key Text: Psalm 55:22

"Cast your cares on the Lord, and he will sustain you; he will never let the righteous fall."

Key Text: Isaiah 40:31

"But they that wait upon the LORD shall renew their strength; they shall mount up with wings as eagles; they shall run, and not be weary, and they shall walk, and not faint."

Key Text: Romans 15:13

"May the God of hope fill you with all joy and peace as you trust in him, so that you may overflow with hope by the power of the Holy Spirit."

Action Plan: Part A

Memorize/Meditate on the Bible verses

Ask yourself what does the verse mean to me?

How can you apply it to my life?

Action Plan: Part B: Reflection Time

What was the experience like?

Thoughts _____

Feelings _____

Actions _____

Ending Prayer: In this prayer, you are pouring your heart out to God, letting Him know all your thoughts, feelings and desires. Pray His words back to Him. In other words, wrestle with God to apply victory to your life.

Keep reciting the key text throughout the day.

"But they that wait upon the LORD shall renew their strength; they shall mount up with wings as eagles; they shall run, and not be weary, and they shall walk, and not faint."

Evening Worship at your desired time: Repeat the process.

Sample #4: Addictions

Name: Paul
Dates: January 18, 2018
Morning Practice: 7 am
Evening Practice: 8 pm

Start with a short prayer:

Example: Lord, thank you for waking me this morning. Open my mind as I seek to worship you. Send your Holy Spirit to guide and teach me your ways and your desires for my life. Give me strength and wisdom from meditating on your Words. In your keep and care, I commit my life, my struggles, and my ultimate victory. In Jesus` Name. Amen.

Two Christian Songs:

Hymns such as:

1. "Take my life and let it be consecrated Lord to Thee."
2. "All to Jesus I surrender, All to Him I freely give" will be appropriate.

Read your Bible

Key Text: Titus 2:12

"It teaches us to say "No" to ungodliness and worldly passions, and to live self-controlled, upright and godly lives in this present age."

Key Text: 1 Corinthians 10:13-14

"No temptation has overtaken you except what is common to humanity. And God is faithful; he will not let you be tempted beyond what you can bear. But when you are tempted, he will also provide a way out so that you can endure it."

Dr. Courtney Dookie

Key Text: Philippians 2:13

"For God is working in you, giving you the desire and the power to do what pleases him."

Action Plan: Part A

Memorize/Meditate on the Bible verses

Ask yourself what does the verse mean to me?

How can you apply it to my life?

Action Plan: Part B: Reflection Time

What was the experience like?

Thoughts   _____

Feelings   _____

Actions   _____

Ending Prayer: In this prayer, you are pouring your heart out to God; let Him know all your thoughts, feelings and desires. Pray His words back to Him. In other words, wrestle with God to apply victory to your life.

Keep reciting key text throughout the day.

"No temptation has overtaken you except what is common to humanity. And God is faithful; he will not let you be tempted beyond what you can bear. But when you are tempted, he will also provide a way out so that you can endure it."

Evening Worship at your desired time: Repeat the process.

REFERENCES

Aas, M., Kauppi, K., Brandt, C. L., Tesli, M., Kaufmann, T., Steen, N. E., Melle, I. (2017). Childhood trauma is associated with increased brain responses to emotionally negative as compared with positive faces in patients with psychotic disorders. *Psychological medicine*, 669–679.

Adolphs, R. (2010). What does the amygdala contribute to social cognition? *Academic science*, 42–61.

Agency for Healthcare Research and Quality. (2009). Mental Health Research Findings. Agency for Healthcare Research and Quality.

Ainsworth, M. S., & Bowlby, J. (1991). An ethological approach to Personality development. *American psychologist*, 333-341.

Alisic, E., Boeije, H. R., Jongmans, M. J., & Kleber, R. J. (2011). Supporting children after single-incident trauma: Parent's review. *Clinical pediatrics*

Allen, M., Diatz, M., Blair, K. S., van Beek, M., Rees, G., Vestergaard-Poulsen, P., . . . Roepstorff, A. (2015). Cognitive-affective neural plasticity following active-controlled mindfulness intervention. *Neuroscience*, 15601-15610.

American Psychiatric Association. (2013). *Diagnostic and Statistical Manual of Mental Disorder*. (5, Ed.) Washington: American Psychiatric publishing.

American Psychological Association. (2015). *Publication manual of the American psychological association.* Washington, DC: American Psychological Association.

Andrew, N., & Iversen, J. (2003). The neural basis of the complex task of meditation: neurotransmitter and neurochemical considerations. *Med hypotheses,* 282-291.

Awasthi, B. (2013). Issues and perspective in meditation research: In search a definition. *Frontiers in psychology.*

Azari, N. P., Nickel, J., Wunderlich, G., Niedeggen, M., Hefter, H., Tellmann, L., . . . Seitz, R. (2014). Short communication: Neural correlates of religious experience. *European Journal of Neuroscience,* 1649–1652.

Balch, M. S., & Loomis, J. (2017). Enhancing care models to Capture psychological trauma. *Journal of Psychosocial Nursing.*

Barnum, E. L., & Perrone-McGovern, K. M. (2017). Attachment, self-esteem and subjective well-being among survivors of childhood sexual trauma. *Journal of Mental Health Counseling,* 39-55.

Beebe, B., Lechmann, F., Markees, S., Buck, K. A., Bahrick, L. E., Chen, H., . . . Jaffe, J. (2012). On the origin of disorganized attachment and internal working models: Paper II. An empirical microanalysis of 4-mouth mother-infant interaction. *Psychological Dialogues,* 352-374.

Berg-Johansen, H., & Duzel, E. (2016). *Neuroplasticity: Effects of physical and cognitive activity of brain structure and function.* Elsevier, 1-3.

Berkovich-Ohana, A., Glicksohn, J., & Goldstein, A. (2012). Mindfulness-induced changes in gamma band activity-implications for the default mode network, self-reference and attention. *Clinical Neurophysiological,* 700-710.

Berlucchi, G., & Buchtel, H. A. (2009). Neuronal plasticity: historical roots and evolution of meaning. *Exp brain res,* 1611-1616.

Bishop, S. R., Lau, M., Shapiro, S., Carlson, L., Anderson, N. D., & Carmody, J.(2004). Mindfulness: a proposed operational definition. *Clinical Psychological Science Practice*, 230-241.

Bloom, D. E., Cafiero, E. T., Jane-Liopis, E., Abrahams-Gessel, S., Bloom, L. R., Fathima, S., . . . Weinstein, C. (2011). The global economic burden of non-communicable diseases. *Harvard School of Public Health*. World economic forum.

Bond, K., Ospina, M. B., Hooton, N., Bialy, L., Dryden, D. M., Buscemi, N., . . . Carlson, L. E. (2009). Defining a complex intervention: The development of demarcation criteria for meditation. *Psychology religion and spirituality, 1*(2), 129-137.

Braboszcz, C., Cahn, B. R., Balakrishnan, B., Maturi, R. K., Grandchamp, R., & Delorme, A. (2013). Plasticity of visual attention in Isha yoga meditation practitioners before and after a 3-month retreat. *Frontiers in Psychology*.

Brand, C., Draper, C., England, A., Bond, S., Clendenen, E. R., Butler, T. C., & Latta, B. (2004). *Holman Illustrated Bible Dictionary*. Nashville: Holman bible publishers.

Bremner, J. D. (2007). Traumatic stress: effects on the brain. *Dialogues in Clinical Neuroscience*, 445-461.

Brewer, J. A., Worhunsky, P. D., Grey, J. R., Tang, Y.-Y., Weber, J., & Kober, H. (2011). Meditation experience is associated with differences in default mode network activity and connectivity. *PNAS*.

Brown, F., Driver, S., & Briggs, C. (2008). *The Brown-Drivers-Briggs Hebrews and English lexicon*. Massachusetts: Hendrickson publishers, Inc.

Burkhart, L. M., & Rasmussen, H. F. (2017). Parental mentalizing as an indirect link between parenting and satisfaction. *Journal of Family Psychology*, 203-213.

Cahn, R. B., Goodman, M. S., Peterson, C. T., Maturi, R., & Mills, P. J. (2017). Yoga, meditation and mind-body health: Increased BDNF, cortisol awakening response and altered inflammatory marker expression after a 3-month yoga and meditation retreat. *Frontiers in Human Neuroscience.*

Cahn, R. B., & Polich, J. (2006). Meditation states and traits: EEG, ERP, and neuroimaging studies. *Psychology bulletin.*

Calabrese, F., Rossetti, A. C., Racagni, G., Gass, P., Riva, M. A., & Molteni, R. (2014). Brian-derived neurotrophic factors: a bridge between inflammation and neuroplasticity. *Frontiers in Cellular Neuroscience.*

Canadian Mental Health Association. (2016, April 03). Fast facts about mental illness. Retrieved from Canadian Mental Health Association: http://www.cmha.ca/media/fast-facts-about-mental-illness/#.WOLbGLEZOuU

Cassidy, J., Jones, J. D., & Shaver, P. R. (2013). Contributions of attachment theory and research: A framework for future research, translation, and policy. *Department of Psychopathology*, 1415-1434.

Catanzaro-Barrasso, C., & Eslinger, P. J. (2016). Neurobiological bases of executive function and social-emotional development: Typical and atypical brain changes. *Interdisciplinary Journal of Applied Family Studies*, 108-119.

Cheng, A., Hou, Y., & Mattson, M. P. (2010). Mitochondria And neuroplasticity. *Neurology.*

Christopher, J. C., Wendt, D. C., Goodman, D. S., & Marecek, J. (2014). Critical cultural awareness: Contributions of a globalizing psychology. *American Psychology*, 645-655.

Cloitre, M., Stolbach, B. C., Herman, J. L., van der Kolk, B., Pynoos, R., Wang, J., & Petkova, E. (2009). A developmental approach to complex PTSD: Childhood and adult cumulative trauma as predictors of symptom complexity. *Journal of Traumatic Stress*, 1-10.

Cloitre, M., Stovall-McClough, K., Nooner, K., Zorbas, P., Cherry, S., Jackson, C., . . . Petkova, E. (2010). Treatment for PTSD related to childhood abuse: A randomized controlled trial. *American Journal of Psychiatry*, 915-924.

Cook, A., Spinazzola, J., Ford, J., Lanktree, C., Blaustein, M., Cloitre, M., . . van der Kolk, B. (2005). Complex trauma in children and adolescents. *Psychiatric Annals*, 390-398.

Courtois, C. A., & Ford, J. D. (2013). *Treatment of complex trauma: A sequenced, relationship-based approach*. New York: The Guilford Press.

Craigmyle, N. A. (2013). The beneficial effects of meditation: contribution of the anterior cingulate and locus coeruleus. *Frontiers in Psychology*.

Dackis, M. N., Rogosch, F. A., Oshri, A., & Cicchetti, D. (2012). The role of limbic system irritability in linking history of childhood maltreatment and psychiatric outcomes in low- income, high-risk Women: Moderation by FKBP5. *Developmental Psychopathology*,1237-1252.

Davidson, R. (2008). Buddha's brain: Neuroplasticity and meditation. *IEEE Signal Process Magazine*, 176-174.

Davidson, R. J. (2016). The four keys to well-being. Mindfulness and well-being at work. New York: *Greater Good: The science of a meaningful life*.

Davis, J. J. (2012). *Meditation and communion with God: Contemplating Scripture in an Age of Distraction*. Downers Grove: InterVarsity Press.

De Bellis, M. D., & Zisk, A. (2015). The biological effects of childhood trauma. *Child Adolescence Psychiatric Clinical Neuroscience*, 185-222.

De Bellis, M. D., Spratt, E. G., & Hooper, S. R. (2011). Neurodevelopmental biology associated with childhood sexual abuse. *Child Sex Abuse*, 548-587.

Dr. Courtney Dookie

Debbane, M., Salaminios, G., Luyten, P., Badoud, D., Armando, M., Tozzi, A., . . . Brent, B. (2016). Attachment, neurobiology, and mentalizing along the psychosis continuum. *Frontiers in Human Neuroscience*.

Desbordes, G., Negi, L. T., Pace, T. W., Wallace, A. B., Raison, C. L., & Schwartz, E. L. (2012). Effects of mindful-attention and compassion meditation training on amygdala response to emotional stimuli in an ordinary, non, meditative state. *Frontiers in Human Neuroscience*.

Dorjee, D. (2016). Defining contemplative science: The metacognitive self-regulatory capacity of the mind, context of meditation practice and modes of existential awareness. *Frontiers Psychology*.

Duhig, P. M., Connell, S., Foley, M., Capra, C., Dark, F., Gordon, A., . . . Scott, J. (2015). The prevalence and correlates of childhood trauma in patients with early psychosis. *Aust N Z J Psychiatry*, 651-659.

Ed, S. (2017, April 03). Mental illness remains taboo topic for many pastors. Retrieved from LifeWay Research: http://lifewayresearch.com/2014/09/22/mental-illness-remains-taboo-topic-for-many-pastors/

Eifring, H. (2013). Meditation in Judaism, Christianity and Islam: Technical aspects of devotional practices.

Enlow, M. B., Egeland, B., Carlson, E., Blood, E., & Wright, R. J. (2014). Mother-infant attachment and the intergenerational transmission of posttraumatic stress disorder. *Developmental Psychopathological*, 41-65.

Ereshefsky, M. (2013). *The poverty of the linemen hierarchy: A Philosophical study of biological taxonomy*. Cambridge: Press Syndicate.

Felita, V. J., Anda, R. F., Nordenberg, D., Williamson, D. F., Spitz, A. M., Edwards, V., . . . Marks, J. S. (1998). Relationship of childhood abuse and household dysfunction to many of the leading causes of death in adults. The adverse childhood experiences (ACE) study. *American Journal of Preventive Medicine*, 14.

Fernando, G., & Kristy, F. (2016). Adapting mindfulness for conservative Christians. *Journal of Psychology and Christianity.*

Finkelhor, D. (2008). *Childhood victimization: violence, crime, and abuse of young people.* New York: Oxford university press.

Flahertly, E. G., Thompson, R., Dubowitz, H., Harvey, E. M., English, D. J., Everson, M. D., . . . Runyan, D. J. (2014). Adverse childhood experiences and child health in early adolescence. *JAMA Pediatrics,* 622-629.

Flaherty, S. C., & Sadier, L. S. (2011). A review of attachment theory in the context of adolescent parenting. Journal of Pediatric Health Care, 114-121.

Folco, S. D., Messina, S., Zavattini, G. C., & Psouni, E. (2017). Attachment to mother and father at transition to middle childhood. *Journal of Child and Family Studies,* 721-733.

Ford, J., van der Kolk, B. A., Spinazzola, J., D'Andrew, W., & Stolback, B. (2012). Understanding interpersonal trauma in children: Why we need a developmentally appropriate trauma diagnosis. *American Journal of Orthopsychiatry,* 187-200.

Ford, J. D., Grasso, D., Greene, C., Levine, J., Spinazzola, J., & van der Kolk. (2013). Clinical significance of a proposal developmental trauma disorder diagnosis: Results of an international survey of clinicians. *Journal of Psychiatry,* 841-849.

Friston, K. J., & Frith, C. D. (2015). *Active inference, communication and hermeneutics.* Elsevier. Fryers, T., & Brugha, T. (2013). Childhood determinates of adult psychiatric disorder. *Clinical Practice Epidemiology Mental Health,* 1-50.

Grisw(word, S. (2014). Comparison of biblical and Buddhist meditation with reflections on mission. *Journal of Adventist Mission Studies, 10*(1).

Dr. Courtney Dookie

Grossman, F. K., Zucker, M., Spinazzola, J., & Hopper, E. (2017). Treating adult survivors of childhood emotional abuse and neglect: A new framework. *American Journal of Orthopsychiatry*, 86-93.

Hackett, C., & Grim, B. (2011). Global Christianity: A report on the size and distribution of the world's Christian population. The pew forum onreligion and public life. Pew Research Center.

Han, S., Mao, L., Gu, X., Zhu, Y., Ge, J., & Ma, Y. (2008). Neural consequences of religious beliefs on self-referential processing. *Social Neuroscience*, 1-15.

Harris, S., Kaplan, J. T., Curiel, A., Bookheimer, S. Y., Iacoboni, M., & Cohen, M. S. (2009). The Neural correlates of religious and nonreligious. *Plos One*.

Hayward, R. D., Owen, A. D., Koenig, H. G., Steffens, D. C., & Payne, M.E. (2011). Association of religious behavior and experiences with extent of regional atrophy in the orbitofrontal cortex during older adulthood. *Religion Brain Behavior*, 103-118.

Holzen, B. K., Carmody, J., Vangel, M., Congleton, C., Yerramsetti, S. M., Gard, T., & Lazar, S. W. (2011). Mindfulness practice leads to increase in reginal brain grey matter density. *Psychiatry Research*, 36-43.

Hofmann M., Stefan, Grossman Paul, Hinton E., Devon (2015). Loving-Kindness and Compassion Meditation: Potential for Psychological Interventions.

Howlett, J. R., & Paulus, M. P. (2015). The neural basic of testable and non-testable beliefs. *PLOS One*.

Infurna, F. J., Rivers, C. T., Reich, J., & Zautra, A. J. (2015). Childhood trauma and personal mastery: Their influence on emotional reactivity to everyday events in a community sample of middle-aged adults. *Plos one*, 1-21.

Jones, J. D., & Cassidy, J. (2014). Parental attachment style: Examination of likes with parent secure base provision and adolescent secure base use. *Attachment Human Development*, 437-461.

Kabat-Zinn, J. (2003). Mindfulness-based interventions in context: past, present, and future. Clinical Psychological Science Practice, 144-156.

Kapogiannis, D., Barbey, A. K., Su, M., Zamboni, G., Krueger, F., & Grafman, J. (2009). Cognitive and neural foundation of religious belief. PNAS, 4876-881.

Kira, I. A., Alawneh, A. N., Aboumediane, S., Mohanesh, J., Ozkan, B., & Alamia, H. (2011). Identity salience and its dynamics in Palestinian adolescents. Scientific research, 781-791.

Kolassa, I.-T., & Elbert, T. (2007). Structural and functional neuroplasticity in relation to traumatic stress. Current Direction in Psychological Science, 321-325.

Kumar, S., Nagendra, H., Naveen, K. V., Manjunath, N. K., & Telles, S. (2010). Brainstem auditory-evoked potentials in two meditative mental states. International Journal of Yoga, 37-41.

Kurth, F., Graham-Mackenzie, A., toga, A. W., & Luders, E. (2015). Shifting brain asymmetry: the link between meditation and structural lateralization. Social Cognitive Affective Neuroscience, 55-61.

Landers, M. S., & Sullivan, R. M. (2012). The development and neurobiology of infant attachment and fear. Developmental Neuroscience, 101-114.

Larsson, S., Andreassen, A. O., Ass, M., Rossberg, I. J., Mork, E., Steen, E. N., . . . Lorentzen, S. (2013). High prevalence of childhood trauma in patients with schizophrenia spectrum and affective disorder. Comp Psychiatry, 123-127.

Leung, M.-K., Chan, C. C., Yin, J., Lee, C.-F., So, K.-F., & Lee, T. M. (2013). Increased grey matter volume in the right angular and posterior Para hippocampal gyri in loving-kindness meditators. Social Cognitive Affective Neuroscience, 34-39.

Lifeway Research. (2014). Mental illness remains taboo topic for many pastors. Lifeway Research.

Luders, E., Clark, K., Narr, K. L., & Toga, A. W. (2011). Enhanced brain connectivity in long-tern meditation practitioners. *Neuroimaging*, 1308-1316.

Luders, E., Kurth, F., & Thompson, P. M. (2015). Larger hippocampal dimensions in meditation practitioners: differential effects in women and men. *Frontier in Psychology*, 186.

Luders, E., Toga, A. W., Lepore, N., & Gaser, C. (2009). The underlying anatomical correlates of long-term meditation: larger hippocampal and frontal volumes of grey matter. *Neuroimage*, 672-678.

Lutz, A., Slagter, H., Dunne, H., & Davidson, R. (2008). Attention regulation and monitoring in meditation. *Trends in Cognitive Science*, 163-169.

Lyons-Ruth, L., Pechtel, P., Yoon, S. A., Anderson, C. M., & Teicher, M. H. (2016). Disorganized attachment in infancy predicts greater amygdala volume in adulthood. *Behavior Brain Research*, 83-93.

Mandell, D. (2014). *The Adverse childhood experiences study: How are the findings being applied in Oregon?* Rose: The Ford Family Foundation.

Malinowski, P. (2013). Neural mechanisms of attention control in mindfulness meditation. *Frontiers in Neuroscience*.

Margo, L. S., & Sullivan, R. M. (2012). The development and neurobiology of infant attachment and fear. *Developmental Neuroscience*, 101-114.

Marcinniak, R., Sheardova, K., Cermakova, P., Hudecek, D., Sumec, R., & Hort, J. (2014). Effects of meditation on cognitive functions in context of aging and neurodegenerative disease. *Frontiers in Behavioral Neuroscience*.

Marusak, H. A., Kuruvadi, N., Vila, A. M., Shattuck, D. W., Joshi, S. H., Joshi, A. A., . . . Thomason, M. E. (2016). Interactive effects of BDNF val66met genotype and trauma on limbic anatomy in childhood. *European Child Adolescent Psychiatry*, 509-518.

McEwen, B. S., Nasca, C., & Gray, J. D. (2016). Stress effects on neuronal structure: Hippocampus, amygdala, and prefrontal cortex. *Neuropsychopharmacology*, 3-23.

Miller, L., Bansal, R., Wickramaratne, P., Hao, X., Tenke, C., Weissman, M. M., & Peterson, B. S. (2014). Neuroanatomical correlates of religiosity and spirituality. *JAMA Psychiatry*, 128-135.

Mohandas, E. (2008). Neurobiology of Spirituality. *MSM*, 63-80.

Munivenkatappa, A., & Agrawal, A. (2016). Role of thalamus in recovery of traumatic brain injury. Journal of Neurosciences in Rural Practice, 76-79.

Nash, J. D., & Newberg, A. (2013). Toward a unifying taxonomy and definition for meditation. *Frontiers in Psychology*, 1-17.

Newberg, A. B., Wintering, N., Waldman, M. R., Amen, D., Khalsa, D., & Alavi, A. (2010). Cerebral blood flow difference between long-term meditators and non-meditators. *Consciousness and cognition*.

Newberg, A. B. (2014). The neuroscientific study of spiritual practices. *Frontiers in Psychology*, 1-6.

Newberg, A. (2016). How God changes your brain: An introduction to Jewish neuroethology. *CCAR Journal: The Reform Jewish Quarterly*.

Ogla, C. M., Rubin, D. C., & Siegler, I. C. (2015). The relation between insecure attachment and posttraumatic stress: Early life versus adulthood traumas. *Psychological Trauma*, 324-332.

Pascual-Leone, A., Amedi, A., & Merabet, L. B. (2005). The plastic human brain cortex. *Annual Review Neuroscience*, 377-401.

Peres, J. F., Giommi, F., & Gielen, S. C. (2012). Neuroimaging during trance state: a contribution of the study of dissociation. *PLOS ONE*.

Perry, B. D. (2012). Stress, trauma, and post-traumatic stress disorders in children. *The Child Trauma Academic*.

Perry, B. D. (2014). Helping traumatized children: A brief overview for caregivers. *Child Trauma Academy.*

Perry, C., Riege, A., & Brown, L. (1999). Realism's role among scientific paradigms in marketing research. 15-22.

Perry, R., & Sullivan, R. M. (2014). Neurobiology of attachment to an abusive caregiver: Short-term benefits and long tern costs. *Developmental Psychobiology,* 1626-1634.

Pignatelli, M., Umanah, G. K., Ribeiro, S. P., Dawson, V. L., Dawson, T. M., & Bonci, A. (2017). Synaptic plasticity onto dopamine neurons shapes fear leering. *Neuron Article,* 425-440.

Planalp, E. M., & Braungart-Rieker, J. M. (2014). Temperamental precursors of infant attachment with mothers and fathers. *Infant Behavior Development,* 36.

Quirin, M., Gillath, O., Pruessner, J. C., & Eggert, L. (2010). Adult attachment insecurity and hippocampal cell density. *SCAN,* 39-47.

Read, J., Fosse, R., Moskowitz, A., & Perry, B. (2014). The traumagenic neurodevelopmental model of psychosis revised. *Neuropsychiatry,* 65-79.

Sar, V. (2011). Developmental trauma, complex PTSD, and the current proposal of DSM-5. *European Journal of Psychopharmacology.*

Sargeant, J. (2012). Qualitative research part II: Participants, analysis, and quality assurance. *Journal Graduate Medicine Education,* 1-3.

Schopen, A., & Freeman, B. (1992). Meditation: The forgotten western tradition. *Counseling and Values.*

Seleh, A., Potter, G. G., McQuoid, D. R., Boyd, B., Turner, R., MacFall, J. R., & Tayler, W. D. (2017). Effects of early life stress on depression, cognitive performance and brain morphology. *Psychological Medicine,* 171-181.

Short, E. B., Kose, S., Mu, Q., Borckardt, J., Newberg, A., George, M. S., & Kozel, F. A. (2010). Regional brain activation during meditation shows time and practice effects: An explanatory FMRI study. Evidence-based *Complementary and Alternative Medicine*, 121-127.

Siegel, D. J. (2012). Pocket guide to interpersonal neurobiology. NY: W.W. Norton & Company, Inc.

Siegel, D. J. (2011). Toward an interpersonal neurobiology of the developing mind: Attachment relationship, "mindsight," and neural interaction. *Attachment and Neurobiology*, 67-94.

Singleton, O., Holzel, B., Vangel, M., Brach, N., Carmody, J., & Lazar, S. W. (2014). Change in brainstem grey matter concentration following a mindfulness-base intervention in correlated with improvement in psychological well-being. *Frontier in Human Neuroscience*.

Sperry, L. (2016). Trauma, neurobiology, and personality dynamic: A primer. *Journal of Individual Psychology*.

Stephens, M. C. (2012). Stress and the HPA Axis: Role of glucocorticoids in alcohol dependence. *Alcohol Research*, 468-483.

Substance abuse and mental health services administration. (2015). Trauma and violence. Retrieved from Substance abuse and mental health services administration: https://www.samhsa.gov/trauma-violence

Sullivan, R. M. (2012). The neurobiology of attachment to nurturing and abusive caregivers. *Hasting Law Journal*, 1553-1570.

Sullivan, R. M. (2012). The neurobiology of attachment to nurturing and abusive caregivers. *Hasting Law Journal*, 1553-1570.

Supin, J. (2016, Nov). The long shadow: Bruce Perry on the lingering effects of childhood trauma. *The Sun*, 4-13.

Tang, Y.-Y., Holzel, B. K., & Posner, M. I. (2015). The neuroscience of mindfulness meditation. *Nature Reviews Neuroscience*, 213-225.

Tang, Y.-Y., Lu, Q., Fan, M., Yang, Y., & Posner, M. I. (2012). Mechanisms of white matter changes induced by meditation. *PNAS*, 10570-10574.

Tang, Y.-Y., Lu, Q., Geng, X., Stein, E. A., Yang, Y., & Posner, M. I. (2010). Short-term meditation induces white matter changes in the anterior cingulate. *PNAS*, 15649-15652.

Tang, Y.-Y., Rothbart, M. K., & Posner, M. I. (2012). Neural correlates of establishing, maintaining, and switching brain states. *Trends in Cognitive Science*.

Travis, F., & Shear, J. (2010). Focused attention, open monitoring and automatic self-transcending: Categories to organize meditations from Vedic, Buddhist and Chinese traditions. *Conscious Cognition*, 1110-1118.

van der Kolk, B. (2003). The neurobiology of childhood trauma and abuse. *Child and Adolescent Psychiatric Clinics*, 293-317.

van der Kolk, B. (2008). Developmental trauma disorder: A new, rational diagnosis for children with complex trauma histories. *Psychiatric Annals*.

van der Kolk, B. A., & Pynoos, R. S. (2009). Proposal to include a developmental trauma disorder diagnosis for children and adolescents in DSM-V.

Wells, R. E., Yeh, G. Y., Kerr, C., Wolkin, J., Davis, R. B., Tan, Y., . . . Kong, J. (2013). Meditation's impact on default mode network & hippocampus in mild cognitive impairment: a pilot study. *Neuroscience Letters*, 15-19.

Yamamoto, T., Toki, S., Siegle, G. J., Takamura, M., Takaishi, Y., Yosimura, S., . . . Yamawaki, S. (2017). Increased amygdala reactivity following early life stress: a potential resilience enhancer role. *BMC Psychia*.

Yyrka, A. R., Burgers, D. E., Noah, B. A., Phillip, S., Lawrence, P. H., & Carpenter, L. L. (2013). The Neurobiological correlates of childhood adversity and implications for treatment. *Acta psychiatry scand*, 434-447.

AUTHOR BIOGRAPHY

Dr. Dookie is a Registered Provisional Clinical Psychologist. He is passionate about helping individuals find true transformation and renewing of their minds. He is the founder of Mind Renewal Ministry and currently serves as a clinical psychologist with his wife in their private practice Dookies' Psychological Services in Northern Alberta.

He has his Doctoral degree in Clinical Psychology, with an emphasis in developmental trauma. He achieved his BA in Theology at Northern Caribbean University, Jamaica and MA in Spiritual Care and Psychotherapy at Wilfrid Laurier University, Canada. Dr Dookie has been providing individuals and couples therapy since 2012. He specializes in developmental trauma and addiction therapy (substance use, gambling addiction, gaming addiction, pornography addiction), and mental health therapy (PTSD, depression, anxiety, eating disorder). Other supports he

Dr. Courtney Dookie

provides include self-esteem, stress management, anger management, holistic counselling (physical, emotional and spiritual).

Dr. Dookie is a speaker, and mentor who does workshops and seminars on the following topics: How God designs the mind, parenting your child's mind, healing the mind and brain through biblical meditation, how prayer transforms the mind, God's plan to restore the mind, and the ten principles for mind growth. He is the author of two books, Neuroplasticity: Healing the Brain from Psychological Disorders through Biblical Meditation and Christian Contemplative Meditation Practice: How Biblical Contemplative Practice Facilitates Neuroplasticity in Adults who have Experienced Developmental Trauma.

Printed in the United States
By Bookmasters